30-Minute Suppers

INTRODUCTION

You love food and want to feed your family and yourself well, but like so many of us, time is not always on your side in the kitchen. Which is why you will find this book your saviour. We've cast our culinary net wide to catch quick meal ideas from all over the world. In these recipes you will find inspiration for any day of the week or occasion.

In the time it takes to heat up a ready meal or dial a takeaway, you can have a fresh meal on the table. Home-cooked food is best nutritionally and financially. With these speedy suppers you're in control!

Each recipe has been tried and tested for taste and reliability. The reputation of Good Housekeeping means you can relax as you get cooking, and have fun!

SALADS

There are more salad ingredients in supermarkets and on market stalls than ever before. A dizzying range of exotic lettuce and leaves from around the world are now available, and all the year round too. This is just as well as doctors and the media regularly recommend that we eat more fruit and vegetables. While it doesn't take much effort to make a salad into a proper meal, we all need some inspiration from time to time. These recipes offer a wide variety of salads to choose from.

CHICKEN, AVOCADO AND PEANUT SALAD

2tbsp cider vinegar

1 level tsp English ready-made mustard

5tbsp groundnut oil

1 large ripe avocado, stoned, peeled and thickly sliced

2 roasted chicken breasts, about 250g (9oz) total
   weight, skin removed, and sliced

70g bag watercress

50g (2oz) roasted salted peanuts, roughly chopped

serves 4

preparation time: 15 minutes, plus chilling

per serving: 400 cals, 34g fat, 2g carbohydrate

Roasted peanuts add an unusual twist to this easy salad dish. *Illustrated.*

1 Put the cider vinegar, mustard and groundnut oil together in a bowl, season with salt and freshly ground black pepper and whisk until well emulsified. Add the avocado and gently toss in the dressing, making sure each slice of avocado is well covered.

2 Arrange the sliced chicken breasts on top of the watercress, cover with clingfilm and chill.

3 Just before serving, spoon the avocado and dressing over the chicken and watercress. Sprinkle with the chopped, roasted peanuts and serve immediately.

CHINESE PRAWN NOODLE SALAD

3 × 150g (5oz) packs of 'straight to the wok' medium
   egg noodles

2tbsp runny honey

2tbsp dark soy sauce

2tbsp rice wine vinegar

4tbsp sesame oil

2 red chillies, deseeded and finely chopped

4 spring onions, finely sliced

½ cucumber, halved, deseeded and finely diced

2 × 160g packs cooked king prawns, preferably
   coriander and chilli flavoured

1 level tbsp chopped fresh coriander

serves 4

preparation time: 15 minutes, plus chilling and
   5 minutes soaking

per serving: 400 cals, 16g fat, 43g carbohydrate

Prawn noodles don't have to be hot – serve this salad lightly chilled.

1 Put the noodles in a bowl and pour over boiling water to cover. Whisk the honey, soy sauce, vinegar and oil together with some black pepper. Drain the noodles and, while still warm, pour over the dressing. Toss together, then allow to cool.

2 To serve, stir the chillies, spring onions, cucumber, prawns and coriander into the noodles and pile into a large bowl. Serve lightly chilled.

HUMMUS WITH ROCKET AND MINT SALAD

400g can chickpeas, drained and rinsed

juice of 1 lemon

4tbsp tahini

1 garlic clove, crushed

5tbsp extra-virgin olive oil for the dressing

3tbsp sherry vinegar

6 tbsp extra-virgin olive oil

TO SERVE

3 × 50g bags wild rocket

12 small mint leaves

12 peppadew sweet piquant peppers (mild)

6 level tbsp sliced jalapeño chillies

4 sesame seed flatbreads, toasted and cut into three

serves 6

preparation time: 15 minutes

cooking time: 5 minutes

per serving: 470 cals, 31g fat, 39g carbohydrate

Set your tastebuds tingling with this great combination: hummus, piquant peppers, flatbreads, chillies and a simply dressed salad. *Illustrated.*

1 Put the chickpeas, lemon juice, tahini, garlic and olive oil in a food processor. Season generously with salt and freshly ground black pepper, then whiz to a paste.

2 Spoon the hummus into a non-metallic bowl, then cover and chill overnight.

3 For the dressing, put the sherry vinegar, olive oil and a pinch of salt in a screwtop jar. Tighten the lid and shake well to mix. Chill overnight.

4 To serve, divide the hummus between six small (150ml/5fl oz) pots. Put on to six plates. Put the rocket and mint leaves in a bowl, then drizzle the dressing over. Divide the salad, peppers, jalapeño chillies and sesame flatbreads among the six plates.

tip: *Once the salad is dressed, you need to serve the starter within 20 minutes.*

TROUT, TOMATO AND LEMON SALAD

4 ripe tomatoes, preferably vine ripened, sliced

caster sugar to sprinkle

5 level tbsp crème fraîche

2 level tbsp horseradish cream

2 level tbsp dill and mustard sauce

grated zest of 1 lemon and 2tbsp lemon juice

2 × 135g packs smoked trout fillets, flaked

4 thick slices country-style bread, toasted

1 little gem lettuce, broken into small leaves

1 thin-skinned lemon, peeled and very thinly sliced, to garnish

serves 4

preparation time: 20 minutes

per serving: 545 cals

per serving: 320 cals, 13g fat, 30g carbohydrate

Smoked trout on toasted doorsteps – the perfect comfort food.

1 Put the tomatoes on a plate and season with a little sugar, salt and freshly ground black pepper. Cover and put to one side.

2 Put the crème fraîche, horseradish cream, dill and mustard sauce, lemon rind and juice in a large bowl, then whisk together and season.

3 Add the smoked trout to the crème fraîche mixture and toss together. Arrange the tomatoes on the toast and spoon any tomato juice over. Arrange the lettuce and trout mixture on top of the tomatoes, garnish with lemon and serve.

CRISP GREEN SALAD WITH BLUE CHEESE DRESSING

100g (3½oz) Roquefort

2tbsp low-fat natural yogurt

1tbsp white wine vinegar

5tbsp extra-virgin olive oil

2 baby cos or 2 hearts of romaine lettuce

50g (2oz) croutons

serves 4

preparation time: 15 minutes

per serving: 310 cals, 29g fat, 7g carbohydrate

This delicious salad only needs six ingredients and takes 15 minutes to prepare. *Illustrated.*

1 To make the dressing, put half the Roquefort into a food processor, add the yogurt, vinegar and oil and whiz for 1 minute until combined. Season with salt and freshly ground black pepper.

2 Separate the lettuce leaves, wash in cold water and dry in a salad spinner or on kitchen paper. Arrange in a shallow dish, tearing any large leaves in two, and scatter the croutons over. Pour over the dressing and crumble over the remaining Roquefort.

PEAR, GRAPE AND PARMESAN SALAD

1tbsp white wine vinegar

½ level tsp Dijon mustard

3tbsp walnut oil

1tbsp sunflower oil

125g (4oz) white seedless grapes, halved

2 large ripe pears, peeled, cored and thickly sliced

2 × 70g bags rocket, washed and dried

175g (6oz) Parmesan cheese shavings

50g (2oz) walnut pieces

serves 4

preparation time: 15 minutes, plus 15minutes
   marinating

per serving: 450 cals, 34g fat,17g carbohydrate

This classic Italian combination makes a refreshing summer salad.

1 Put the vinegar, mustard and oils in a small bowl. Season with salt and freshly ground black pepper, then whisk together until thoroughly emulsified.

2 Put the grapes and pears into a bowl, pour the dressing over and toss together. Leave to marinate for 15 minutes.

3 At the last minute, tear the rocket into smallish pieces, put in a large bowl, add the grape mixture and toss together. Serve the salad topped with the Parmesan cheese shavings and the walnut pieces.

PARMA HAM, MARINATED ONION AND ROCKET

150g (5oz) small marinated onions, drained, reserving
  1tbsp of the marinade
4tbsp olive oil
200g (7oz) bag of rocket
8 slices Parma ham, about 100g (3½oz)
75g (3oz) Parmesan cheese shavings

serves 4
preparation time: 7–8 minutes
per serving: 300 cals, 25g fat, 4g carbohydrate

This is a classic Italian salad. Look out for ready-made marinated onions in major supermarkets. *Illustrated.*

1 To make the dressing, place the reserved marinade, olive oil, salt and freshly ground black pepper in a bowl and whisk together until combined.
2 Halve the onions and put in a large bowl with the rocket, Parma ham, Parmesan shavings and the dressing. Toss together and serve at once.

GRAVADLAX WITH CUCUMBER SALAD

1 small cucumber, halved, deseeded and thinly sliced
3tbsp white wine vinegar
1 level tbsp caster sugar
3 level tbsp chopped fresh dill
2 × 125g packs gravadlax with dill and mustard sauce
4tbsp crème fraîche
12 mini blinis (15g each)
dill sprigs to garnish

serves 4
preparation time: 15 minutes, plus 15 minutes
  marinating
per serving: 270 cals, 10g fat, 27g carbohydrate

Sweet and sour cucumber, sour crème fraîche – delicious.

1 Arrange the sliced cucumber on a large plate. Mix together the white wine vinegar, caster sugar and chopped fresh dill, then season to taste with salt and freshly ground black pepper. Pour the dressing over the cucumber and marinate for 15 minutes.
2 Mix the dill and mustard sauce into the crème fraîche and season with salt and freshly ground black pepper.
3 Lightly toast the mini blinis. Arrange the marinated cucumber on four individual serving plates with the slices of gravadlax, the crème fraîche sauce and the blinis. Garnish with dill sprigs and serve.

TOMATO, MOZZARELLA AND BASIL SALAD WITH BALSAMIC DRESSING

2tbsp balsamic vinegar

4tbsp extra-virgin olive oil

25g (1oz) pine nuts

3 ripe beef tomatoes, sliced

125g pack buffalo mozzarella, drained and torn into
   bite-sized pieces

15 small basil leaves

serves 4

preparation time: 15 minutes

per serving: 260 cals, 24g fat, 2g carbohydrate

This delicious salad only needs six ingredients and takes 15 minutes to prepare. *Illustrated.*

1 To make the dressing, put the balsamic vinegar and oil in a small bowl, whisk together and season generously with salt and freshly ground black pepper.
2 Put the pine nuts into a dry frying pan and toast, stirring, for 3 minutes. Set aside for a few minutes to cool.
3 Arrange the tomatoes and mozzarella on a large plate or shallow dish, season and drizzle with the dressing. Scatter the pine nuts and basil on top and serve.

PEPPERED MACKEREL SALAD

250g pack vacuum-packed beetroot, diced

1tbsp olive oil

2tsp white wine vinegar

2 × 170g pots potato salad

1–2tbsp lemon juice

4 smoked mackerel peppered fillets, skinned and
   flaked

2 level tbsp chopped fresh chives

chives to garnish

serves 4

preparation time: 15 minutes

per serving: 460 cals, 36g fat, 18g carbohydrate

Peppered mackerel fillets are great for no-cook fish dishes.

1 Put the diced beetroot in a bowl, sprinkle with the olive oil and white wine vinegar. Season with salt and freshly ground black pepper and toss together.
2 Put the potato salad in a large bowl and mix with the lemon juice. Season to taste with salt and ground black pepper. Add the flaked smoked mackerel and chopped chives and toss together.
3 Pile the mackerel mixture into a large bowl just before serving, sprinkle the diced beetroot over the top of the salad and garnish with the chives.

THAI SALAD

200g (7oz) sugarsnap peas, trimmed

250g packet of Thai stir-fry rice noodles

100g (3½oz) cashew nuts

300g (11oz) carrots, cut into batons

10 spring onions, sliced on the diagonal

300g bag beansprouts

20g bunch coriander, roughly chopped

1 red bird's eye chilli, deseeded and finely chopped

2 level tsp sweet chilli sauce

4tbsp sesame oil

6tbsp soy sauce

juice of 2 limes

serves 4–6

preparation time: 20 minutes

cooking time: 7–8 minutes

per serving for 4: 600 cals, 29g fat, 71g carbohydrate

per serving for 6: 400 cals, 19g fat, 47g carbohydrate

Rice noodles are so easy to use – just cover them with boiling water and leave to soak for a few minutes. Here, the noodles are tossed with sugarsnaps, beansprouts, toasted cashew nuts, coriander, carrots and a spicy chilli dressing for a satisfying salad. *Illustrated.*

1 Bring a pan of salted water to the boil and blanch the sugarsnaps for 2–3 minutes until just tender to the bite. Drain and refresh under cold water.

2 Prepare the noodles: put them in a bowl and cover with boiling water. Leave to soak for 4 minutes, rinse under cold water and drain very well.

3 Toast the cashews in a dry frying pan until golden – around 5 minutes.

4 Put the sugarsnaps in a large glass serving bowl. Add the carrots, spring onions, beansprouts, coriander, chilli, cashews and noodles. Mix together the chilli sauce, sesame oil, soy sauce and lime juice and season well. Pour over the salad and toss together.

PASTA, SALAMI AND TAPENADE SALAD

3 x 225g pots of pasta salad

70g pack pepper salami, shredded

3 level tbsp black olive tapenade paste

3 level tbsp chopped fresh chives

serves 4

preparation time: 5 minutes

per serving: 380 cals, 24g fat, 34g carbohydrate

Mix pre-made pasta salad with salami and an olive tapenade – easy!

1 Turn the pasta salad into a large bowl, add the salami, the olive tapenade and the chives. Toss everything together and season with freshly ground black pepper. Check for seasoning before adding salt – the tapenade may have made the salad salty enough.

2 Pile into a large bowl and serve. This salad is best kept in a cool place, but not chilled, before serving.

SPINACH, AVOCADO AND BACON SALAD WITH MUSTARD DRESSING

1 level tbsp wholegrain mustard

juice of ½ lemon

6tbsp extra-virgin olive oil

12 smoked streaky bacon rashers

200g (7oz) baby leaf spinach, washed and ready to use

1 large ripe avocado, stoned, peeled and sliced

serves 4

preparation time: 15 minutes

per serving: 530 cals, 50g fat, 1g carbohydrate

A classic salad ready in 15 minutes. *Illustrated.*

1 To make the dressing, put the mustard, lemon juice and olive oil in a small bowl and whisk together. Season with salt and freshly ground black pepper.

2 Preheat the grill. Lay the bacon rashers on a wire rack in a grill pan, then grill for 4–5 minutes until golden and crisp. Drain on kitchen paper, cool, then cut into pieces with scissors.

3 Tip the spinach into a large bowl. Scatter the bacon and avocado slices on top, then drizzle the mustard dressing over. Carefully toss everything together before serving.

CHICKEN AND WATERCRESS SALAD

4 slices of stale bread, cubed

2tbsp olive oil

100g (3½oz) watercress

heads of chicory, leaves separated

4 ready-roasted chicken breasts, sliced

1 large ripe avocado, stoned, peeled and sliced

FOR THE DRESSING

50g (2oz) Roquefort cheese, chopped

1tbsp white wine vinegar

2tbsp natural yogurt

5tbsp olive oil

serves 4

preparation time: 10 minutes

cooking time: 10 minutes

per serving: 600 cals, 42g fat, 21g carbohydrate

An ideal supper for a warm summer's evening. Just mix together ready-roasted chicken breasts, peppery watercress, chicory and croutons, and top with an easy blue cheese dressing.

1 Preheat the oven to 200°C (180°C fan oven) mark 6. Put the bread on a baking tray and drizzle with olive oil. Season well with salt and freshly ground black pepper, then toss to make sure all the cubes are well coated in oil. Bake in the oven for 10 minutes until golden brown.

2 To make the salad dressing, put the cheese in a bowl. Add the vinegar, yogurt and olive oil and season to taste. Mix together well, then set aside.

3 To assemble the salad, put the watercress in a large bowl and add the chicory leaves, sliced chicken and avocado. Scatter over the croutons and drizzle over the blue cheese dressing before serving.

WARM CHICKEN LIVER SALAD

1–2tbsp balsamic vinegar

1 level tsp Dijon mustard

5tbsp olive oil

2 × 225g tubs chicken livers

200g (7oz) streaky bacon rashers, deirinded, cut into
small pieces (lardons)

½ curly endive, about 175g (6oz)

100g (3½oz) rocket

1 bunch spring onions, sliced

serves 4

preparation time: 20 minutes

cooking time: 8–10 minutes

per serving: 520 cals, 43g fat, 2g carbohydrate

Unless you have very good, aged balsamic vinegar for this dressing it's best to put 2tbsp of the vinegar in a small pan and reduce it by half. This will give the dressing a nice mellow flavour. You can save time by buying bacon lardons, which most supermarkets now sell. *Illustrated.*

1 To make the dressing for the salad, put the balsamic vinegar, mustard, 4tbsp of the olive oil, salt and freshly ground black pepper in a small bowl. Whisk together and put to one side.

2 Drain the chicken livers, then trim and cut into pieces.

3 In a non-stick frying pan, fry the lardons until beginning to brown, stirring from time to time. Add the remaining oil and the chicken livers and stir-fry over a high heat for 2–3 minutes or until just pink in the centre. Season with salt and freshly ground black pepper.

4 Toss the endive, rocket and spring onions with the dressing in a large bowl. Quickly combine the warm livers and bacon and serve at once.

LOCAL MARKET SALAD

2 large ripe avocados, stoned, peeled and sliced into
eight lengthways

300g (11oz) small tomatoes on the vine, cut in half

1 fennel bulb, thinly sliced

100g (3½oz) feta cheese, diced

50g (2oz) small pepperoni sausage – or any other spicy
sausage – thinly sliced

plenty of cress or 1 bunch of watercress

75ml (3fl oz) salad dressing – either our easy
two-minute dressing, right, or a good quality
ready-made one

serves 4

preparation time: 15 minutes

per serving: 380 cals, 35g fat, 5g carbohydrate

You should be able to buy these ingredients at any market, but don't worry if you have to find substitutes for one or two. It will still taste delicious and it'll be on the table in minutes.

1 Put the avocados in a large salad bowl. Add the tomatoes, fennel, feta, pepperoni and cress or watercress.

2 Drizzle over the dressing, then toss carefully and serve.

two-minute dressing: Put 2tbsp vinegar into a jam jar with 4tbsp olive oil and 1½tsp mustard (Dijon or wholegrain). Screw the jar shut and shake to emulsify.

WARM OYSTER MUSHROOM AND SPINACH SALAD

4 slices focaccia bread, cut into cubes

2tbsp balsamic vinegar

1 level tsp Dijon mustard

3tbsp sunflower oil

6tbsp walnut oil

225g (8oz) streaky bacon rashers, de-rinded
   and cut into short, thin strips

350g (12oz) oyster mushrooms

25g (1oz) walnut pieces

450g (1lb) baby spinach, washed and dried

serves 4

preparation time: 20 minutes

cooking time: 8 minutes

per serving: 840 cals, 71g fat, 25g carbohydrate

**Serve as a starter, or with cooked chicken, ham or salmon
as a main course. *Illustrated.***

1 Bake the focaccia cubes at 200°C (180°C fan oven) mark
6 for 6–8 minutes or until lightly toasted.

2 Whisk together the vinegar, mustard, salt and freshly
ground black pepper in a small bowl, until combined; then
whisk in the sunflower oil and half the walnut oil. Put to
one side.

3 Cook the bacon in a non-stick frying pan for 2–3 minutes,
add the remaining walnut oil and heat for 1 minute, then add
the mushrooms. Stir-fry the mixture over a brisk heat for 2–3
minutes or until wilted and the bacon is brown and crisp. Take
the pan off the heat, stir in the walnut pieces and season to
taste with salt and freshly ground black pepper.

4 Put the spinach in a large bowl, add the bacon and
mushrooms and toss together with the dressing. Pile into a
serving dish and sprinkle with the focaccia croûtons. Serve
the salad immediately.

CHICKPEA SALAD WITH LEMON AND PARSLEY DRESSING

juice of ½ lemon

6tbsp extra-virgin olive oil

4 level tbsp chopped flat-leafed parsley, plus extra
   sprigs to garnish

2 x 410g cans chickpeas, drained and rinsed

1 small red onion, finely sliced

serves 4

preparation time: 15 minutes

per serving: 350 cals, 23g fat, 25g carbohydrate

**Only five ingredients are needed to make this delicious
salad meal.**

1 To make the dressing, put the lemon juice, oil and parsley
in a medium bowl and whisk together. Season generously
with salt and freshly ground black pepper.

2 Tip the chickpeas into a large salad bowl, add the red
onion and drizzle the dressing over. Mix together well and
taste to check the seasoning. Set aside for 5 minutes to allow
the onion to soften slightly in the dressing, then serve.

tip: *If you're making lots of salads for a party, make this one
the night before and store it, covered, in the fridge.*

PASTA, RICE AND NOODLES

Of all cooking ingredients, pasta, rice and noodles are the most versatile. Cheap, nourishing and quick to cook, their endless versatility means it's impossible to get fed up with eating them. National cuisines have been built around these simple staple foods. For the cook they offer a more or less blank canvas. So we have brought together a whole palette of ideas for you to draw upon in your cooking. From the operatic gusto of Italian pasta, to the clean, aromatic flavours of the East, here, you will find a meal to suit most occasions, be it a simple lunch, a comforting dinner with friends or a family meal.

PASTA WITH CHILLI AND TOMATOES

350g (12oz) pasta, such as fusilli

4tbsp olive oil

1 large red chilli, deseeded and finely chopped

1 garlic clove, crushed

500g (1lb 2oz) cherry tomatoes

2 level tbsp chopped fresh basil

50g (2oz) freshly grated Parmesan cheese

serves 4

preparation time: 5 minutes

cooking time: 15 minutes

per serving: 720 cals, 36g fat, 78g carbohydrate

Wash your hands carefully after chopping the chilli as it can irritate skin and eyes. *Illustrated.*

1 Bring a large pan of water to the boil. Add the pasta and cook according to packet instructions. Drain.

2 Meanwhile, heat the oil in a large frying pan, add the chilli and garlic and cook for 30 seconds. Add the tomatoes, season with salt and freshly ground black pepper and cook over a high heat for 3 minutes or until the skins begin to split.

3 Add the chopped basil and drained pasta and toss together. Sprinkle the Parmesan shavings over and serve.

PENNE WITH LEEKS AND SALAMI

400g (14oz) penne

150g (5oz) salami, cut into cubes

2 medium leeks, washed and sliced

1 garlic clove, crushed

1tbsp olive oil

100ml (3½fl oz) crème fraîche

handful of flat-leafed parsley, chopped

freshly grated Parmesan cheese to serve

serves 4

preparation time: 6 minutes

cooking time: 8 minutes

per serving: 500 cals, 19g fat, 69g carbohydrate

Cubes of salami and leeks tossed with crème fraîche, pasta and flat-leafed parsley. Delicious!

1 Bring a large pan of water to the boil. Add the penne and cook according to packet instructions.

2 Heat a non-stick pan over a medium heat and fry the salami for 2–3 minutes. There's no need for oil at this point – the heat will release the fat from the meat. Add the leeks and garlic to the pan with the oil and toss to coat. Turn the heat right down, cover and cook for 10 minutes or until soft and translucent.

3 Add the crème fraîche to the pan and season well. Continue to cook on the lowest heat until the sauce is warmed through.

4 Drain the pasta, reserving a little of the cooking water. Tip the pasta back into the pan with the sauce, the parsley and a splash of the reserved water. Toss well to coat. Serve with plenty of grated Parmesan.

CREAMY PARMA HAM AND ARTICHOKE TAGLIATELLE

500g pack dried tagliatelle

500ml carton crème fraîche

280g jar roasted artichoke hearts,
  drained and halved

80g pack Parma ham (6 slices), torn into strips

2 level tbsp chopped fresh sage leaves,
  plus extra leaves to garnish

40g (1½oz) freshly grated Parmesan cheese

serves 4

preparation time: 5 minutes

cooking time: 10 minutes

per serving: 1000 cals, 58g fat, 97g carbohydrate

The easiest way to create a delicious and instant creamy sauce is to add a tub of crème fraîche to pasta, then stir in some special ready-to-use ingredients for a luxurious combination that even non-cooks can achieve. *Illustrated.*

1 Bring a large pan of water to the boil. Add the pasta, cover and bring back to the boil, then remove the lid, turn the heat down to low and simmer according to the instructions on the pack.

2 Drain well, reserving some of the cooking water, then put the pasta back in the pan.

3 Add the crème fraîche, artichoke hearts, Parma ham and chopped sage and stir everything together, thinning with a ladleful of the cooking water. Season well with salt and freshly ground black pepper.

4 Spoon the pasta into warmed bowls, sprinkle the freshly grated Parmesan cheese over each portion and garnish with sage leaves. Serve immediately.

SPAGHETTI WITH ANCHOVIES

350g (12oz) spaghetti

2tbsp olive oil

400g can red pimentos, drained

50g (2oz) anchovy fillets, drained and chopped

3 level tbsp chopped flat-leafed parsley

serves 4

preparation time: 5 minutes

cooking time: 10–12 minutes

per serving: 430 cals, 11g fat, 71g carbohydrate

Use dried spaghetti rather than fresh.

1 Cook the spaghetti according to packet instructions. Drain, return to the pan and add the remaining ingredients. Mix together well, season with freshly ground black pepper and serve.

SMOKED BACON PAPPARDELLE

200g (7oz) smoked lardons (or smoked rindless
   back bacon, chopped)
350g packet dried egg pappardelle
500ml carton crème fraîche
1 level tbsp fresh or sundried sage leaves, torn
50g (2oz) freshly grated Parmesan cheese

serves 4
preparation time: 5 minutes
cooking time: 15 minutes
per serving: 1040 cals, 75g fat, 68g carbohydrate

This creamy pasta dish takes just five ingredients.

1 Heat a non-stick frying pan and dry-cook the lardons or bacon for 4 minutes or until brown and crisp. Drain on kitchen paper.

2 Bring a large pan of salted water to the boil, add the pappardelle and return to the boil. Cook according to the packet instructions. Drain the pasta and reserve some of the cooking liquid.

3 Tip the crème fraîche into the warm pan and heat through for 3 minutes with the sage. Add 4tbsp of cooking liquid. Return the pasta to the pan and toss with the crème fraîche and crisp bacon. Season generously with freshly ground black pepper, and sprinkle in the grated Parmesan. Serve immediately with a tomato salad.

tip: *If the pasta absorbs all the creamy sauce when you return it to the pan, add 2tbsp more of the reserved pasta water and stir in.*

feeding a latecomer *Reserve a quarter each of pan-fried lardons, uncooked pappardelle, crème fraîche, sage and Parmesan. When needed, bring a large pan of water to the boil and cook the pappardelle according to packet instructions. Heat lardons in a frying pan and stir in crème fraîche and sage. Toss with pasta, sprinkle with Parmesan and season with salt and freshly ground black pepper.*

HERB, LEMON AND CRISPY CRUMB PASTA

3 level tbsp chopped flat-leafed parsley

8 level tbsp chopped fresh basil

grated zest of 1 lemon plus 2tbsp juice

200ml tub crème fraîche

1tbsp olive oil

4 level tbsp fresh breadcrumbs

350g (12oz) pasta, such as fusilli

serves 4

preparation time: 5 minutes

cooking time: 8–12 minutes

per serving: 540 cals, 25g fat, 70g carbohydrate

A traditional Sicilian dish perfect for warm summer evenings. *Illustrated.*

1 Mix together the herbs, lemon rind and juice and the crème fraîche in a large bowl. Season well with salt and freshly ground black pepper.

2 Heat the olive oil in a frying pan and fry the breadcrumbs for 5 minutes or until golden brown. Drain on absorbent kitchen paper and put to one side.

3 Meanwhile, cook the pasta in a large pan of boiling salted water, according to the packet instructions. Drain well, return the pasta to the pan, stir in the crème fraîche mixture and heat through. Sprinkle over the fried breadcrumbs and serve at once.

SPECIAL PRAWN FRIED RICE

1tbsp sesame oil

6 level tbsp nasi goreng paste

250g (9oz) cooked king prawns

200g (7oz) green cabbage, shredded

2 × 250g packs of microwave rice

2tbsp soy sauce

1tbsp sunflower oil

2 eggs, beaten

2 spring onions, finely sliced

1 lime, halved

serves 4

preparation time: 5 minutes

cooking time: 8–10 minutes

per serving: 380 cals, 15g fat , 43g carbohydrate

This is a fantastic midweek supper based on an Indonesian dish called nasi goreng. There are many variations but they're all served with a shredded omelette on the top. Use a ready-made paste and a pack of microwaveable rice for speed.

1 Heat the sesame oil in a wok and fry the nasi goreng paste for 1–2 minutes. Add the prawns and cabbage, and fry for 2–3 minutes. Next add the rice and soy sauce, and cook for a further 5 minutes, stirring occasionally.

2 To make the omelette, heat the sunflower oil in a nonstick frying pan (around 25.5cm/10in in diameter) and add the eggs, Swirl around to cover the base in a thin layer and cook for 2–3 minutes until set.

3 Roll up the omelette and cut it into slivers. Serve the rice scattered with the egg and spring onions, and pass around the lime halves to squeeze over.

MUSHROOMS AND GREEN BEANS WITH NOODLES

25g (1oz) butter

1 tbsp olive oil

1–2 garlic cloves, peeled and crushed

1 lemongrass stalk, finely chopped

1 medium red chilli, deseeded and chopped

250g (9oz) fine green beans, trimmed

250g pack dried egg noodles

150g (5oz) shiitake mushrooms, trimmed

150g (5oz) oyster mushrooms, halved if large

4 level tbsp roughly chopped fresh coriander,
   plus extra leaves to garnish

1 lemon, cut into wedges, to serve

serves 4

preparation time: 15 minutes

cooking time: 15 minutes

per serving: 320 cals, 10g fat, 50g carbohydrate

Lemongrass adds a tang to this filling dish of noodles tossed in a buttery sauce and spiked with garlic and chilli. *Illustrated.*

1 Put the butter and oil in a wok or large frying pan and heat gently to melt the butter. Add the crushed garlic, lemongrass and chilli and stir-fry for around 30 seconds.

2 Bring a large pan of water to the boil and steam the green beans for 5 minutes. Remove the steamer and use the water to cook the noodles, according to the instructions on the packet. Drain well.

3 Add the green beans and both types of mushroom to the frying pan or wok and stir-fry for 3–4 minutes. Add the noodles and coriander and toss everything together. Garnish with coriander leaves and serve in warmed bowls with the lemon wedges.

WALNUT AND CREAMY BLUE CHEESE TAGLIATELLE

400g (14oz) tagliatelle

1 tsp olive oil

1 garlic clove, crushed

25g (1oz) walnut pieces, toasted

100g (3½oz) Gorgonzola, chopped into cubes

142ml carton single cream

50g (2oz) rocket

serves 4

preparation time: 5 minutes

cooking time: 10–12 minutes

per serving: 550 cals, 26g fat, 60g carbohydrate

Pasta ribbons are best served with a creamy sauce that will cling to them. This is another classic, with Gorgonzola, walnuts, cream and peppery rocket.

1 Bring a large pan of water to the boil. Add the tagliatelle and cook according to the packet instructions.

2 A few minutes before the pasta is ready, make the sauce. Heat the olive oil in a small pan, add the garlic and walnuts, and cook for 1 minute – the garlic should be just golden. Add the Gorgonzola and cream, and season with a little salt and plenty of freshly ground black pepper.

3 Drain the pasta well and return to the pan with a couple of spoonfuls of cooking water. Add the creamy sauce and rocket. Toss well and serve immediately.

VEGETABLE AND SAFFRON RISOTTO

1 large courgette, chopped

1 each yellow and red pepper, deseeded and chopped

600ml (1 pint) vegetable stock

175g (6oz) flat mushrooms, chopped

generous pinch saffron strands

250g (9oz) risotto rice

1 bunch spring onions, trimmed and finely sliced

2 tomatoes, deseeded and chopped

freshly grated Parmesan cheese, shredded basil
    and basil leaves to garnish

serves 2 as a main course or 4 as an accompaniment

preparation time: 8 minutes

cooking time: 30 minutes

per serving for 2: 610 cals, 9g fat, 110g carbohydrate

per serving for 4: 310 cals, 4g fat, 55g carbohydrate

Risotto is a great quick supper – this one is creamy and velvety, yet low in fat. Although the preparation time takes the total over 30 minutes, the vegetables could be prepared in advance. *Illustrated.*

1 Put the courgette and peppers in a large pan, add the stock and bring to the boil. Simmer for 5 minutes. Add mushrooms and simmer for a further 5 minutes. Drain and reserve the stock. Add the saffron.

2 Cook the risotto rice, according to the packet instructions, in the reserved stock.

3 When the rice is tender – 18–20 minutes – stir in the cooked vegetables, spring onions and tomatoes. Season generously with salt and freshly ground black pepper. Garnish with the Parmesan and basil to serve.

THAI NOODLES WITH PRAWNS

4–6 level tsp Thai red curry paste

175g (6oz) medium egg noodles,
    preferably wholewheat

2 small red onions, chopped

1 stalk lemon grass, trimmed and sliced

1 Thai red chilli, deseeded and finely chopped

300ml sachet low-fat coconut milk

400g (14oz) raw tiger prawns, peeled

4 level tbsp chopped fresh coriander

torn coriander to garnish

serves 4

preparation time: 10 minutes

cooking time: 5 minutes

per serving: 340 cals, 11g fat, 38g carbohydrate

Ready-made prawn crackers make a fast and easy accompaniment to this dish.

1 Put 2 litres (3½ pints) boiling water in a large pan, add the Thai red curry paste, noodles, onions, lemon grass, chilli and coconut milk. Bring to the boil, add the prawns and chopped coriander. Simmer for 2–3 minutes or until the prawns turn pink. Season to taste with salt and freshly ground black pepper.

2 Serve in large bowls sprinkled with the torn coriander.

tip: *Don't overcook, or the noodles will become mushy and the prawns tough.*

feeding a latecomer: *Reserve a quarter of the uncooked noodles and prawns and 1 level tbsp fresh coriander. Remove a ladleful of the cooking liquid, including a few pieces of onion, lemon grass and chilli. Cover and keep cool. When needed, bring the liquid to the boil in a pan, add the noodles and prawns and simmer for 2–3 minutes. Pour into a bowl and top with a sprinkling of coriander.*

PASTA WITH BROCCOLI AND THYME

500g packet dried rigatoni pasta

900g (2lb) tenderstem broccoli, ends trimmed, or
   2 broccoli heads, chopped into florets and stalks
   peeled and sliced

150ml (¼ pint) hot vegetable stock

2 garlic cloves, crushed

2tbsp olive oil

250g tub mascarpone

2 level tbsp chopped fresh thyme

100g (3½oz) freshly grated pecorino cheese

serves 4

preparation time: 15 minutes

cooking time: 15 minutes

per serving: 950 cals, 48g fat, 100g carbohydrate

This is a super-easy, foolproof midweek supper. Broccoli is cooked until tender, then tossed with garlic, thyme, mascarpone and pecorino (an Italian sheep's milk cheese) to make a creamy sauce for the pasta.

1 Bring a large pan of salted water to the boil, add the pasta, cover with a lid and bring to the boil again. Remove the lid, stir the pasta and cook according to the timings on the pack. Drain well, reserving about a ladleful of the cooking water.

2 Meanwhile, make the sauce: put the broccoli in a pan with the stock. Bring to the boil, then cover with a lid and simmer for 3–4 minutes until tender – the stock should have evaporated. Add the garlic and olive oil and cook for 1–2 minutes to soften the garlic. Add the mascarpone, thyme and pecorino and carefully mix together.

3 Return the pasta to the pan, then add the broccoli sauce. Toss everything together, adding a little of the reserved cooking water if necessary, then season to taste with salt and freshly ground black pepper. Divide among four warmed pasta bowls and enjoy!

PASTA WITH CREAMY PESTO SAUCE

5 level tbsp freshly grated Parmesan cheese

25g (1oz) pinenuts, toasted

200g carton low-fat fromage frais

2 garlic cloves

40g (1½oz) torn fresh basil leaves

40g (1½oz) roughly chopped fresh parsley

450g (1lb) fresh tagliatelle

serves 4

preparation time: 8 minutes

cooking time: 5 minutes

per serving: 460 cals, 14g fat, 61g carbohydrate

This low-fat version of the classic Italian pasta dish is surprisingly creamy.

1 Put the Parmesan cheese, pinenuts, fromage frais and garlic into a food processor and whiz to a thick paste. Scrape into a bowl and season generously with salt and freshly ground black pepper. Add the herbs and whiz for 2–3 seconds.

2 Cook the pasta according to packet instructions. Drain thoroughly, stir in the pesto sauce and check the seasoning before serving.

SAFFRON AND COCONUT TIGER PRAWN PAPPARDELLE

500g packet pappardelle pasta

1tbsp olive oil

1 red onion, finely chopped

4 garlic cloves, crushed

2 Thai red chillies, deseeded and chopped

150ml (¼ pint) dry white wine

150ml (¼ pint) fish stock

1 level tsp saffron threads

2 × 400ml cans coconut milk

700g (1½lb) tiger prawn tails, shelled

2 level tbsp chopped fresh coriander, plus extra leaves
   to garnish

serves 6

preparation time: 10 minutes

cooking time: 12 minutes

per serving: 560 cals, 19g fat, 65g carbohydrate

Marinated in lime juice, saffron, garlic and chilli and quickly cooked, these tiger prawns make a mouth-watering starter or a light main dish.

1 Cook the pasta in a large pan of boiling salted water, according to the packet instructions. Heat the oil in a large pan and fry the onion until soft. Add the garlic and chillies and cook for 2 minutes. Add the white wine and fish stock, then cook until reduced by half.

2 Add the saffron, coconut milk and prawns, then cook for 5 minutes until the prawns have turned pink and are cooked through. Add the chopped coriander and season with salt and freshly ground black pepper.

3 Drain the pasta, divide among six bowls, pour the sauce over the top and garnish with coriander leaves.

CHOPS, STEAK AND CHICKEN

There is a whole world of ideas here for creating a quick main meal with meat. From the sizzling platters of Mexican fajitas to the succulent perfection of a simple grilled British pork chop. When buying meat, buy the best you can afford, and wherever possible aim for organic meat from your butcher rather than mass-produced meat from the supermarket. You'll taste the difference.

CHICKEN TIKKA WITH COCONUT DRESSING

125ml (4fl oz) crème fraîche

5tbsp coconut milk

4 pitta bread

200g bag mixed salad leaves

2 × 210g packs chicken tikka fillets, sliced

2 spring onions, finely sliced

2 level tbsp mango chutney

15g (½oz) flaked almonds

25g (1oz) raisins

serves 4

preparation time: 10 minutes

per serving: 540 cals, 23g fat, 54g carbohydrate

For a great combination of fruit and nuts, try these pittas packed with almonds, mango and raisins. *Illustrated.*

1 Mix the crème fraîche and coconut milk together in a bowl and put to one side.

2 Split each pitta bread to form a pocket, then fill each pocket with a generous handful of mixed salad leaves. Put the sliced chicken tikka fillets on top of the salad, sprinkle the sliced spring onions over, add the mango chutney, drizzle with the crème fraîche mixture, then top with a sprinkling of flaked almonds and raisins. Serve.

CHICKEN FAJITAS

4 skinless, boneless chicken breasts,
    about 700g (1½lb) total weight, cut into chunky strips

360g jar fajita 2-step season and sauce

1tbsp sunflower oil

1 red pepper, deseeded and sliced

1 bunch spring onions, trimmed and halved

320g packet of eight flour tortillas

150g pot tomato salsa

120g pot guacamole dip

142ml pot soured cream

serves 4

preparation time: 10 minutes

cooking time: 10 minutes

per serving (including dips): 790 cals, 38g fat,
    66g carbohydrate

Half the enjoyment of this dish is that everyone can roll and fill their own tortilla.

1 Put the chicken breasts in a shallow dish, sprinkle with half the seasoning and toss together. Heat the oil in a large non-stick frying pan, add the chicken and cook for 5 minutes or until golden brown and tender.

2 Add the pepper and cook for 2 minutes. Pour in all the sauce, bring to the boil and simmer for 5 minutes or until thoroughly heated. Add a splash of boiling water if the sauce becomes too thick.

3 Stir in the spring onions and cook for 2 minutes.

4 Meanwhile, warm the tortillas in a microwave on High for 45 seconds, or wrap in foil and warm at 180°C (160°C fan oven) mark 4 for 10 minutes.

5 Transfer the chicken to a serving dish, or take the frying pan to the table, along with the tortillas, salsa, guacamole and soured cream. Let everyone grab a tortilla, spoon in some chicken, roll up the tortilla, top with salsa, guacamole and soured cream and indulge!

CHICKEN WITH BLACK EYE BEANS AND GREENS

2 level tsp Jamaican jerk seasoning

4 chicken breasts

1kg (2¼lb) spring greens or cabbage, core removed
   and shredded

2 × 300g cans black eye beans, drained

8tbsp olive oil

juice of 1¼ lemons

serves 4

preparation time: 5 minutes

cooking time: 15 minutes

per serving: 560 cals, 34g fat, 23g carbohydrate

If you use skinless chicken breasts for this recipe, brush them with 1–2tbsp oil before grilling. Jerk seasoning is widely available in major supermarkets.

1 Rub the jerk seasoning into the chicken breasts and sprinkle with salt. Cook under a preheated grill for 15 minutes or until done, turning from time to time.

2 Cook the spring greens or cabbage in boiling salted water until just tender – bringing the water back to the boil after adding the greens is usually enough to cook them. Drain and return to the pan.

3 Add the beans and olive oil and season well with salt and freshly ground black pepper. Heat through and add the juice of one lemon.

4 Slice the chicken and place on the spring greens mixture, then drizzle over the remaining lemon juice and serve.

CHILLI STEAK AND CORN ON THE COB

50g (2oz) butter, softened

1 large red chilli, deseeded and finely chopped

1 garlic clove, crushed

25g (1oz) freshly grated Parmesan cheese

1 level tbsp finely chopped fresh basil

4 corn on the cob, each cut into three

1tbsp olive oil

4 × 150g (5oz) sirloin steaks

serves 4

preparation time: 5 minutes

cooking time: 15 minutes

per serving: 390 cals, 23g fat (of which saturates 12g),
   10g carbohydrate

September is the best season for corn – enjoy it hot with a meaty steak and a Parmesan, basil and chilli butter melted over. *Illustrated.*

1 Put the butter in a bowl and beat with a wooden spoon. Add the chilli, garlic, Parmesan and basil, and mix everything together. Cover and chill to firm up.

2 Meanwhile, bring a large pan of water to the boil. Add the corn, cover to bring back up to the boil, then simmer half-covered for around 10 minutes or until tender. Drain well.

3 Heat a little oil in a large frying pan or griddle and cook the steaks for 2–3 minutes on each side for medium-rare or 4–5 minutes for medium. Divide the corn and steaks among four warm plates and top with the butter. Serve with a mixed green salad.

LAMB WITH SPICY COUSCOUS

2 fillets of lamb, each weighing about 400g (14oz)

5tbsp olive oil

1 medium aubergine, cut into 1cm (½in) dice

1 level tsp ground cumin

½ level tsp ground cinnamon

225g (8oz) couscous

1 large red chilli, deseeded and finely chopped

3 level tbsp chopped fresh mint

75g (3oz) raisins, soaked in hot water and drained

yogurt and mint sprigs to garnish

serves 4

preparation time: 10 minutes

cooking time: 15 minutes

per serving: 750 cals, 35g fat, 57g carbohydrate

Leaving the lamb to rest for 5 minutes allows the juices to set so they don't run out.

1 Trim the lamb fillets, rub in 1tbsp oil and season well with salt and freshly ground black pepper. In a heavy non-stick pan, fry the lamb for 15 minutes, turning regularly. Remove from the pan and leave to rest for 5 minutes.

2 Meanwhile, toss the aubergine in the cumin and cinnamon and fry in 2tbsp oil for 10 minutes or until softened. Prepare the couscous according to the packet instructions.

3 Add the aubergine, chilli, 2 level tbsp mint, the raisins and remaining oil to the couscous. Season well with salt and freshly ground black pepper. Slice the lamb and place on the couscous. Drizzle with yogurt, sprinkle with the remaining chopped mint and mint sprigs and serve.

LAMB WITH BUTTER BEANS AND SPINACH

2tbsp olive oil

1 onion, finely sliced

1 garlic clove, crushed

2 × 400g cans butter beans, drained

200g (7oz) spinach

4 small lamb chops

FOR THE DRESSING

3tbsp low-fat yogurt

2 level tbsp tahini

1 level tsp harissa paste

1 lemon, half juiced and the other half
    cut into wedges to serve

serves 4

preparation time: 5 minutes

cooking time: 12–13 minutes

per serving: 450 cals, 21g fat, 29g carbohydrate

The spicy dressing made from tahini – sesame seed paste – and hot harissa lifts ordinary lamb chops to another level. A side order of butter beans and spinach completes the meal. *Illustrated.*

1 Heat 1tbsp olive oil in a large pan. Add the onion and fry over a medium heat for 10 minutes until soft and golden. Add the garlic, cook for 1 minute, then add the butter beans and spinach, and cook for 1–2 minutes to warm through and wilt the spinach.

2 Meanwhile, brush the lamb chops with a little oil and fry in a separate pan on each side for 3–4 minutes.

3 To make the dressing put the remaining olive oil in a bowl, add the yogurt, tahini, harissa, lemon juice and 2tbsp cold water. Season well and mix everything together.

4 To serve, divide the butter bean mixture among four warmed plates. Top with the lamb chops, add a dollop of dressing and serve with the lemon wedges.

PORK MEDALLIONS IN RED WINE SAUCE

350g (12oz) pork fillet or tenderloin, well trimmed and
  cut diagonally into 1cm (½in) slices
1 level tbsp freshly ground mixed peppercorns
oil-water spray
2 garlic cloves, crushed
1 red onion, chopped
200ml (7fl oz) red wine
300ml (½ pint) chicken stock
1 level tsp redcurrant jelly
2 level tsp Dijon mustard

serves 3–4
preparation time: 10 minutes
cooking time: 20 minutes
per serving for 3: 210 cals, 8g fat, 5g carbohydrate
per serving for 4: 160 cals, 6g fat, 4g carbohydrate
  (does not include couscous)

Delicately flavoured pork is perfectly complemented by a herb couscous.

1 Flatten the pork slightly with a rolling pin and sprinkle the ground mixed peppercorns on both sides.

2 Spray a heavy non-stick frying pan with the oil-water spray and heat until starting to smoke. Brown the pork medallions for 1–2 minutes on each side, then remove from the pan.

3 Lower the heat, add the garlic and onions to the pan, then cover and cook for 5 minutes or until soft. Add the wine, reduce by half, then pour in the stock and bubble for 7–10 minutes or until the sauce has reduced by half.

4 Stir in the jelly and mustard and whisk until combined. Return the pork to the pan, bring the sauce to the boil and simmer for 2–3 minutes or until the pork is cooked and the sauce is syrupy. Season with salt and freshly ground black pepper and serve with herb couscous (below) or 15-minute couscous (see page 131).

herb couscous: Put 175g (6oz) couscous in a large bowl. Bring 300ml (½ pint) vegetable stock to the boil and add to the bowl. Season with salt and freshly ground black pepper. Mix through with a fork, cover with clingfilm and leave in a warm place for 10 minutes. Uncover, add 3–4 level tbsp each chopped flat-leafed parsley and mint, two tomatoes, deseeded and chopped, and check seasoning. Serve with the pork medallions.

PORK WITH FRUIT

1 level tbsp chilli paste or harissa, or a chopped red
   chilli – whatever you can get hold of
4tbsp olive oil
zest and juice of 1 large orange
4 pork chops
2 nectarines or peaches, stoned and chopped

serves 4
preparation time: 10 minutes
cooking time: 10–15 minutes
per serving: 460 cals, 26g fat, 8g carbohydrate

This may sound an odd combination, but don't worry, any stone fruit goes brilliantly with pork.

1 Put the chilli paste or harissa in a small bowl. Add the oil, orange zest and juice, then season well with salt and freshly ground black pepper. Drizzle the mixture over the pork and leave to absorb the flavours.

2 Heat a non-stick frying pan and cook the marinated pork for about 3 minutes on each side or until well browned. Add the remaining marinade to the pan with the chopped nectarines or peaches and bring the liquid to the boil. Cook for a further 4–5 minutes until the pork is cooked through. Serve with rice or couscous.

PORK PITTAS WITH SALSA

1tbsp olive oil
500g (1lb 2oz) pack diced pork
4tbsp spicy seasoning such as Old El Paso Spice Mix
   for Fajitas
4 large pittas
100g tub Greek yogurt

for the salsa
1 red onion, peeled and chopped
1 ripe avocado, stoned, peeled and chopped
4 large tomatoes, roughly chopped
small handful roughly chopped fresh coriander,
juice of 1 lime

serves 4
preparation time: 10 minutes
cooking time: 10 minutes
per serving: 550 cals, 24g fat, 50g carbohydrate

Pork pan-fried in Mexican spices is stuffed into toasted pitta with avocado, red onion, tomato and coriander and topped with a dollop of Greek yogurt. Nothing could be easier – enjoy!

1 Heat the oil in a pan and fry the pork over a medium heat for 3–4 minutes. Add the spicy seasoning mix to the pan and stir to coat the pork, then cook for a further 4–5 minutes until cooked through.

2 Meanwhile, make the salsa. Put the onion in a bowl and add the avocado, tomatoes, coriander and lime juice. Mix well, season to taste and set aside.

3 Toast the pittas until lightly golden, then slit down the side and stuff with the pork, a dollop of salsa and a spoonful of Greek yogurt. Serve immediately.

cook's tip: *Make your own seasoning by mixing 1 crushed garlic clove, 1tsp ground ginger and ½–1tsp cayenne pepper. Toss with the pork and complete the recipe.*

CHICKEN WITH SPICY COUSCOUS

125g (4oz) couscous

1 ripe mango, peeled and cut into 2.5cm (1in) chunks

1tbsp lemon or lime juice

1 × 125g tub fresh tomato salsa

3 level tbsp mango chutney

3tbsp orange juice

2 level tbsp chopped fresh coriander

200g pack chargrilled chicken fillets

4tbsp fromage frais

lime chunks and roughly chopped coriander to garnish

serves 4

preparation time: 15 minutes, plus 15 minutes soaking

per serving (with skin): 300 cals, 9g fat,
   39g carbohydrate

per serving (without skin): 270 cals, 5g fat,
   39g carbohydrate

Use precooked chargrilled chicken fillets for this quick and simple dish. *Illustrated.*

1 Put the couscous in a large bowl, pour over 300ml (½ pint) boiling water, season well and leave to stand for 15 minutes. Put the mango on a plate and sprinkle with the lemon or lime juice.

2 Mix together the tomato salsa, mango chutney, orange juice and coriander.

3 Drain the couscous if necessary. Stir the salsa mixture into the couscous and check the seasoning. Turn on to a large serving dish and arrange the chicken and mango on top. Just before serving, spoon the fromage frais over the chicken and garnish with the lime chunks and chopped coriander.

ROAST CHICKEN WITH LEMON COUSOUS

500g packet couscous

600ml (1 pint) hot chicken stock

zest and juice of 3 lemons

400g can chickpeas

10tbsp chopped fresh flat-leafed
   parsley and coriander

75g (2oz) preserved lemons, chopped

100g (3½oz) unblanched almonds, roughly chopped

8 Medjool dates, halved, stoned and quartered

8tbsp extra-virgin olive oil

1 ready-roasted chicken

serves 6

preparation time: 25 minutes, plus chilling

per serving: 1050 cals, 49g fat, 100g carbohydrate

For a vegetarian alternative, replace the chicken with feta cheese, green olives and garlic.

1 Put the couscous in a large bowl, add the chicken stock, lemon zest and juice. Cover and leave to absorb for 10 minutes. Fluff up with a fork.

2 Drain the chickpeas and add to the couscous with the herbs, preserved lemons, almonds, dates and oil. Mix well, cover and chill.

3 To joint the chicken, use a sharp knife to remove the legs, then slice the breast from either side. Slice off the wings.

4 Spoon the couscous and chicken on to plates. Garnish with extra preserved lemon and flat-leafed parsley, and serve.

BASIL AND LEMON MARINATED CHICKEN

grated zest of 1 lemon and 4tbsp lemon juice

1 level tsp caster sugar

1 level tsp Dijon mustard

175ml (6fl oz) lemon-flavoured oil

4 level tbsp chopped fresh basil

2 × 210g packs roast chicken

2 × 120g bags baby leaf spinach

55g pack crisp bacon, broken into small pieces

serves 4

preparation time: 15 minutes,

   plus 15 minutes marinating

per serving: 650 cals, 58g fat, 2g carbohydrate

You can have roast chicken without going near the oven. *Illustrated*.

1 Put the grated lemon zest, lemon juice, caster sugar, Dijon mustard and oil into a small bowl. Season with salt and freshly ground black pepper. Whisk thoroughly together and add the basil.

2 Remove any bones from the roast chicken, leave the skin attached and slice into five to six pieces. Arrange the sliced chicken in a dish and pour the dressing over, then cover and leave to marinate for at least 15 minutes.

3 Just before serving, lift the chicken from the dressing and put to one side.

4 Put the spinach in a large bowl, pour the dressing over and toss together. Arrange the chicken on top of the spinach and sprinkle with the bacon. Serve immediately.

BEEFSTEAK IN MUSTARD SAUCE

oil-water spray

4 × 175g (6oz) sirloin or fillet steaks, trimmed of all fat

2 large garlic cloves, crushed

150ml (¼ pint) red wine

150ml (¼ pint) beef stock

1 level tbsp Dijon mustard

serves 4

preparation time: 2 minutes

cooking time: 10 minutes

per serving: 230 cals, 8g fat, nil carboydrate

The trick to tender beef is to cook it fast over a high heat – make sure the pan is very hot before adding the steaks. If you like your steak rare, cook the meat for 2–3 minutes each side; for well done, cook it for an extra 2–3 minutes on each side.

1 Spray a non-stick pan with the oil-water spray and heat. Season the steaks with salt and freshly ground black pepper.

2 Sear the steaks on both sides until they're cooked to your liking (see above), then set aside.

3 Put the garlic in the pan and sizzle for 1 minute. Add the wine and stock, stirring and scraping up the brown bits on the bottom of the pan with a wooden spoon. Bring to the boil and simmer for about 2 minutes or until reduced by about half, then stir in the mustard and simmer briskly for a further 1 minute. Pour in any juices that have accumulated under the steaks.

4 Quickly cut the steaks into slices on the diagonal and stir into the simmering mustard sauce before serving.

SPICY GLAZED PORK CHOPS

1 level tbsp curry paste
1 level tbsp mango chutney
a large pinch turmeric
1 tbsp vegetable oil
4 pork loin chops

serves 4
preparation time: 5 minutes
cooking time: 15–18 minutes
per serving: 260 cals, 15g fat, 2g carbohydrate

Don't worry if the pork chops blacken slightly while they're under the grill as this will add to the flavour of the finished dish. Serve with sautéed potatoes and grilled cherry tomatoes. *Illustrated.*

1 Put the curry paste, mango chutney, turmeric and oil in a bowl and mix well. Preheat the grill to high. Put the chops on to a grill rack, season well and brush with half the curry mixture.
2 Grill for 8–10 minutes until golden and slightly charred. Turn the chops over, season again and brush with the remaining curry mixture. Put back under the grill and cook for a further 6–8 minutes until tender and slightly charred.

SPICY THAI CHICKEN SOUP

1 tbsp vegetable oil
1 small onion, sliced
300g (11oz) stir-fry chicken pieces
1–2 level tbsp red Thai curry paste
600ml (1 pint) hot chicken stock
400g can chopped tomatoes
100g (3½oz) sugar snap peas, halved
150g (50z) baby sweetcorn, halved
4 level tbsp copped fresh coriander
grated zest of ½ lime
1 wedge of lime to serve

serves 4
preparation time: 2–3 minutes
cooking time: 17 minutes
per serving: 180 cals, 8g fat, 8g carbohydrate

Sometimes there's nothing more comforting than a bowl of nourishing soup – especially if it has a chilli-hot kick to it. This uses ready-made paste, so it's incredibly easy to make.

1 Heat the oil in a large frying pan or wok. Add the onion and fry for 5 minutes until it begins to soften. Add the chicken and cook for a further 5 minutes until golden brown, then add the.curry paste and fry for a further 1 minute to warm the spices through.
2 Pour in the chicken stock and chopped tomatoes, then simmer for 5 minutes. Add the sugar snap peas and baby sweetcorn and cook for a further 1 minute until the chicken is cooked through. Divide the soup among four warmed bowls, sprinkle with coriander and lime zest, and serve with a wedge of lime.

STEAK WITH TANGY HERB DRESSING

2 level tbsp each chopped flat-leafed
   parsley, fresh mint and basil
2 level tbsp capers, roughly chopped
1 level tsp Dijon mustard
2 garlic cloves, crushed
150ml (¼ pint) olive oil
juice of ½ lemon
2tbsp oil
4 × 150g (5oz) fillet steaks
2 large tomatoes, sliced
8 slices toasted ciabatta

serves 4
preparation time: 8 minutes
cooking time: 12–15 minutes
per serving: 690 cals, 43g fat, 41g carbohydrate

Take the steaks out of the fridge 15 minutes before you're ready to start cooking.

1 To make the herb dressing, put the parsley, mint, basil, capers, Dijon mustard, garlic, olive oil and lemon juice in a small bowl and combine thoroughly using a fork.
2 In a heavy-based frying pan, heat 1tbsp oil and fry the steaks for 3 minutes each side for medium rare, 4–5 minutes for medium. Remove when cooked to your taste, put to one side and keep warm.
3 Wipe out the pan, add the remaining oil and fry the tomatoes quickly on both sides, then season with salt and freshly ground black pepper.
4 Put each steak on a slice of toasted ciabatta with slices of tomato and the dressing drizzled over. Top with a second slice of toasted ciabatta and serve.

CHICKEN WITH PEANUT SAUCE

4 skinless chicken fillets, cut into strips
1 level tbsp ground coriander
2 garlic cloves, finely chopped
4tbsp vegetable oil
2tbsp runny honey

for the peanut sauce
1tbsp vegetable oil
2 level tbsp curry paste
2 level tbsp brown sugar
2tbsp peanut butter
200ml (7fl oz) coconut milk

serves 4
preparation time: 15 minutes, plus 15 minutes
   marinating time
cooking time: 6 minutes
per serving: 550 cals, 37g fat, 16g carbohydrate

If you're making this dish for children, use a mild curry paste.

1 Mix the chicken with the ground coriander, garlic, oil and honey. Leave to marinate for 15 minutes.
2 To make the peanut sauce, heat the oil in a pan, add the curry paste, brown sugar and peanut butter and fry for 1 minute. Add the coconut milk and bring to the boil, stirring all the time, then simmer for 5 minutes.
3 Meanwhile, preheat a wok and, when hot, stir-fry the chicken in batches for 3–4 minutes or until cooked, adding more oil if needed.
4 Serve the chicken on a bed of Thai fragrant rice with chopped coriander, with the peanut sauce poured over.

ITALIAN SAUSAGE STEW

25g (1oz) dried porcini mushrooms

1 onion, sliced

2 garlic cloves, chopped

1 small chilli, chopped

2tbsp olive oil

2 stalks fresh rosemary

300g (11oz) whole rustic Italian salami sausages, such
as salami Milano, cut into 1cm (½in) slices

400g can chopped tomatoes

200ml (7fl oz) red wine

175g (6oz) instant polenta

50g (2oz) butter

50g (2oz) freshly grated Parmesan cheese,
plus shavings to serve (optional)

75g (3oz) Fontina cheese, cubed

serves 4

preparation time: 10 minutes

cooking time: 15 minutes

per serving: 780 cals, 48g fat, 47g carbohydrate

Quick-cook polenta and a chunky salami stew that's ready in the time it takes to grill regular bangers.

1 Put the mushrooms in a small bowl and pour over 100ml (3½fl oz) boiling water. Cook in the microwave on High for 3 minutes 30 seconds. Set aside to cool.

2 Gently fry the onion, garlic and chilli with the olive oil for 5 minutes. Remove the leaves from one rosemary stalk and add to the pan, stirring.

3 Add the salami and fry for 2 minutes on each side or until browned. Chop the mushrooms and add to the pan. Add the tomatoes and wine, then season with black pepper. Simmer uncovered for 5 minutes.

4 Put 750ml (1¼ pints) boiling water and 1 level tsp salt in a pan. Return to the boil and add the polenta. Cook according to the packet instructions. Add butter and both cheeses and mix well.

5 Serve the polenta with Parmesan shavings, if using, and stew, garnished with the remaining rosemary.

PORK WITH ARTICHOKES, BEANS AND OLIVES

2tbsp vegetable oil

2 × 275g (10oz) pork fillets, cut into 1cm (½in) slices

2 level tbsp chopped fresh thyme

8tbsp olive oil

400g can artichoke hearts, drained,
    rinsed and quartered

400g can flageolet beans, drained and rinsed

185g jar pitted green olives, drained and rinsed

juice of 1 lemon

serves 4

preparation time: 5 minutes

cooking time: 5–6 minutes

per serving: 600 cals, 47g fat, 13g carbohydrate

The southern Mediterranean flavours in this recipe combine beautifully with the quickly cooked pork.

1 Heat the vegetable oil in a frying pan and fry the pork for 2 minutes on each side. Add the thyme and season with salt and freshly ground black pepper.

2 Meanwhile, heat the olive oil in a pan, add the artichokes and beans and cook for 3–4 minutes. Add the olives and lemon juice and season with black pepper.

3 Place the pork on top of the artichokes, beans and olives and serve.

FISH AND SHELLFISH

Fresh fish fits perfectly into the life of the fast cook, as it is so quick to cook. More and more people are turning to fish for dinner nowadays – it's low in fat, high in protein and virtually fuss free to prepare. For greater variety, swap around the fish used in the recipes. Smoked trout can be used in place of mackerel for example, or haddock for cod. This is the case with most recipes unless the main focus is a particular fish, like a Dover sole.

COD WITH OLIVE AND TOMATO SALSA

100g (3½oz) pitted black olives, chopped

300g (11oz) tomatoes, skinned, deseeded and
  chopped

3 level tbsp chopped fresh basil

4tbsp olive oil

4 pieces of cod, about 175g (6oz) each

small basil leaves to garnish

serves 4

preparation time: 5 minutes

cooking time: 10 minutes

per serving: 290 cals, 17g fat, 2g carbohydrate

This recipe captures the flavours of southern France. Serve it with garlic mayonnaise, quickly made by adding a crushed garlic clove and a little lemon juice to bought mayonnaise. *Illustrated.*

1 Mix the olives, tomatoes, basil and 2tbsp of the olive oil together. Season with salt and freshly ground black pepper and put to one side.

2 Brush the cod with the remaining oil and season. Cook under a preheated grill for 5–10 minutes, turning once. Check it's just cooked in the centre.

3 Serve with the olive and tomato salsa, garnished with basil leaves, and top with garlic-flavoured mayonnaise.

COD WITH ORIENTAL VEGETABLES

4 × 175g (6oz) thick cod fillets

grated zest of 1 lime

1tbsp each chilli oil and sesame oil

1 red chilli, deseeded and chopped

2 garlic cloves, chopped

8 spring onions, trimmed and sliced

125g (4oz) shiitake mushrooms, sliced

225g (8oz) carrots, cut into strips

300g (11oz) pak choi, chopped

2tbsp soy sauce

serves 4

preparation time: 20 minutes,
  plus 30 minutes marinating;

cooking time: about 6 minutes

per serving: 240 cals, 9g fat, 7g carbohydrate

This is a great recipe for low-cholesterol and low-calorie diet. Although only taking 6 minutes to cooks, there is extra time allowance here for the marinating process, which can be done in advance.

1 Put the cod in a shallow, non-metallic dish. Mix the lime zest with the chilli oil and rub over the fillets. Cover and leave in a cool place for 30 minutes.

2 Heat the sesame oil in a large frying pan, add the chilli, garlic, spring onions, mushrooms and carrots and stir-fry for 2–3 minutes or until the vegetables begin to soften. Add the pak choi and stir-fry for 1–2 minutes. Add the soy sauce and cook for a further minute. Season and set aside.

3 Grill the cod fillets under a moderately hot grill for 2–3 minutes on each side or until the flesh has turned opaque and is firm to the touch.

4 Pile the stir-fried vegetables on top of the cod and serve.

DOVER SOLE WITH PARSLEY BUTTER

2 Dover soles, about 275g (10oz) each,
   cleaned and descaled

3 level tbsp plain flour

2 tbsp sunflower oil

25g (1oz) unsalted butter

2 level tbsp chopped flat-leafed parsley

juice of 1 lemon, plus lemon wedges to serve

serves 2

preparation time: 5 minutes

cooking time: 20 minutes

per serving: 450 cals, 25g fat, 16g carbohydrate

Cooking fish on the bone keeps all the flavour and makes it easy to serve. *Illustrated.*

1   Rinse the fish under cold water, then gently pat them dry with kitchen paper. Put the flour on a large plate and season with salt and freshly ground black pepper. Dip the fish into the seasoned flour, to coat both sides, gently shaking off excess.

2   Heat 1tbsp of the oil in a large sauté pan or frying pan and fry one fish for 4–5 minutes on each side until golden. Transfer to a warmed plate and keep warm in a low oven. Add the remaining oil to the pan and cook the other fish in the same way; put on a plate in the oven to keep warm.

3   Add the butter to the pan and melt. Turn up the heat slightly until it turns golden, then take off the heat. Add the parsley and lemon juice, then season well. Put one fish on each warmed dinner plate and pour over the parsley butter. Serve with lemon wedges.

GARLIC AND THYME FISH STEAKS

2 garlic cloves, crushed

2 level tbsp chopped fresh thyme leaves

4tbsp olive oil

2 lemons

4 × 200g (7oz) firm fish steaks, such as tuna,
   swordfish or shark

serves 4

preparation time: 10 minutes, plus 20 minutes
   marinating

cooking time: 5–10 minutes

per serving: 390 cals, 21g fat, nil carbohydrate

Marinating the fish first in lemon juice and oil really tenderizes it. If you're cooking indoors, a griddle pan is a great replacement.

1   Light the barbecue, if you're using one, and let the coals burn to a white ash. Or preheat a griddle pan until searing hot.

2   Put the garlic, thyme, olive oil and the juice of one lemon in a large shallow container and mix together well.

3   Add the fish steaks and season with salt and freshly ground black pepper, then cover and chill for 20 minutes. Cut the other lemon into four slices and put to one side.

4   Cook the fish on the barbecue, or griddle pan, for 4–5 minutes on one side and brush over a little of the marinade. Turn the fish over, put a slice of reserved lemon on top of each steak and continue to cook for 3–4 minutes or until cooked through.

LUXURY SALMON FISHCAKES

butter to grease

1 tbsp olive oil

½ small red onion, finely chopped

700g (1½lb) salmon fillet, skinned,
    cut into 2cm (¾in) cubes

3 level tbsp chopped fresh dill

juice of ½ lemon

serves 6

preparation time: 10 minutes

cooking time: 10–15 minutes

per serving: 260 cals, 18g fat, 1g carbohydrate

Red onion, dill and a squeeze of lemon transform salmon fillet into a stunning dish that's ideal for entertaining.

1 Preheat the oven to 200°C (180°C fan oven) mark 6. Grease a baking sheet and six 9cm (3½in) cooking rings. Or make your own from tin foil: cut out a 30 × 10cm (11¾ × 4in) piece of foil and fold in half lengthways. Wrap the foil around the base of a wine bottle and fold the ends together to secure. Slip the foil ring off the bottle end and repeat to make five more rings. Butter the rings inside.

2 Heat the olive oil in a frying pan and cook the onion for 5 minutes. Tip the onion into a bowl, add the salmon, dill and lemon juice and season well with salt and freshly ground black pepper.

3 Put the cooking rings (or foil rings) on a baking sheet, fill them with the salmon mixture and cook in the oven for 10–15 minutes until firm.

JUICY PRAWNS

250g (9oz) uncooked, shelled tiger prawns

50g (2oz) butter, plus extra to spread on toast

2 level tbsp capers

20g pack coriander, roughly chopped

2 limes, 1 juiced and 1 cut into wedges to serve

8 slices sourdough bread

serves 4

preparation time: 5 minutes

cooking time: 5 minutes

per serving: 500 cals, 23g fat, 55g carbohydrate

Prawns cook in minutes and their fresh sweetness marries perfectly with capers, coriander and zesty lime. *Illustrated.*

1 Prepare the tiger prawns by cutting down the back of each prawn and pulling out the black central vein. Heat the butter in a large frying pan until sizzling, then add the prawns. Fry for 2–3 minutes until they start to turn pink.

2 Add the capers, coriander and lime juice, stirring to coat the prawns, then continue frying until the prawns are cooked through. Serve on toast and buttered sourdough bread with a wedge of lime, making sure everyone has plenty of buttery juices.

OVEN-POACHED COD WITH HERBS

10 spring onions, trimmed and sliced

2 garlic cloves, crushed

6 level tbsp fresh mint, shredded

6 level tbsp chopped flat-leafed parsley

juice of ½ lemon

150ml (¼ pint) fish, chicken or vegetable stock

4 cod fillets, about 200g (7oz) each

lemon wedges to garnish

serves 4

preparation time: 10 minutes

cooking time: 10 minutes

per serving: 160 cals, 2g fat, 1g carbohydrate

Fish is quick to cook, great to eat and the fat levels in cod are very low indeed. *Illustrated.*

1 Combine the spring onions (reserving some of the green part), garlic, mint, parsley, lemon juice and stock in a dish that can just hold the cod in one layer.

2 Put the cod on the herb-garlic mixture and turn to moisten. Season with salt and freshly ground pepper and roast at 230°C (210°C fan oven) mark 8 for 8–10 minutes. Sprinkle with the reserved spring onion, garnish with lemon wedges and serve with mashed potato.

MACKEREL WITH HOT TOMATO SAUCE

2tbsp extra-virgin olive oil

300g punnet cherry tomatoes, halved or,
     if large, quartered

2 level tbsp creamed horseradish

8 uncooked mackerel fillets

small handful rosemary leaves, roughly chopped

serves 4

preparation time: 5 minutes

cooking time: 9–12 minutes

per serving: 540 cals, 40g fat, 4g carbohydrate

The piquant sauce is what makes this dish – cherry tomatoes softened in a pan with extra-virgin olive oil, horseradish and rosemary. Serve with French beans and peas and a wedge of lemon to squeeze over.

1 Preheat the grill to high. Heat 1tbsp of the oil in a wok or large frying pan and fry the tomatoes for 2–3 minutes, tossing them occasionally so they cook quickly and evenly until they start to soften at the edges. Add the creamed horseradish to the pan and toss together to combine. Turn the heat right down, cover and leave to simmer.

2 Meanwhile, brush the mackerel fillets on both sides with the remaining oil and season well with salt and freshly ground black pepper. Grill skin side up for 6–7 minutes until the skin starts to blister and turn golden brown. Turn the fillets over carefully and grill for a further 1–2 minutes.

3 Stir the rosemary into the tomato sauce and spoon it over the mackerel fillets.

cook's tip: *Serve the sauce with smoked mackerel fillets to make this supper even easier.*

SALT-CRUSTED TROUT WITH TARRAGON SAUCE

about 900g (2lb) sea salt

6–8 garlic cloves (unpeeled)

6 level tbsp chopped fresh tarragon

6 trout, cleaned, with heads and tails intact

for the tarragon sauce

500ml carton crème fraîche

1 level tsp Dijon mustard

1 garlic clove, crushed

2 level tbsp chopped tarragon

lemon wedges to serve

serves 6

preparation time: 10 minutes

cooking time: 20 minutes

per serving: 550 cals, 41g fat, 2g carbohydrate

Baking fish in a salt crust is a great way to seal in the natural flavours and keep the fish moist. You can serve the fish cold if you like, but the salt and skin must be removed before chilling, otherwise the fish will taste salty.

1 Line a roasting tin with foil and add enough salt to make a 1cm (½in) layer. Scatter the garlic and about half the tarragon over the salt, then place the fish on top. Press the trout down into the salt, scatter over the remaining tarragon, then cover completely with the remaining salt. Bake at 220°C (200°C fan oven) mark 7 for about 20 minutes.

2 Meanwhile, prepare the sauce. To serve warm, combine all the ingredients except the tarragon in a pan, bring to the boil and simmer for a few minutes, adding the tarragon just before serving. To serve cold, simply mix all the ingredients together in a bowl.

3 Remove the fish from the oven and crack the salt crust open. Carefully lift out the trout on to a board and peel away the skin. Serve with lemon wedges and the tarragon sauce.

BAKED SWORDFISH WITH SUN-DRIED TOMATO PESTO

15g (½oz) pinenuts

2 garlic cloves, roughly chopped

4 level tsp sun-dried tomato paste

15g (½oz) freshly grated Parmesan cheese

½tbsp olive oil

4 × 175g (6oz) swordfish steaks

450g (1lb) courgettes, diced

2tbsp basil oil

250g bag baby spinach leaves

juice of ½ lemon

4 basil leaves to garnish

serves 4

preparation time: 20 minutes

cooking time: 10–15 minutes

per serving: 400 cals, 20g fat, 4g carbohydrate

The pesto topping leaves this meaty fish lovely and moist on the inside. *Illustrated.*

1 Preheat the oven to 200°C (180°C fan oven) mark 6. To make the pesto, put the pinenuts, garlic, tomato paste, Parmesan and olive oil in a blender. Season well and whiz for 30 seconds.

2 Season the fish, divide and press the pesto on to each steak, and put in a roasting tin. Put the courgettes into another roasting tin and drizzle with half the basil oil. Cook both, with the fish on the top shelf, for 10–15 minutes.

3 Put the spinach in a pan. Season, add the lemon juice, and cook until wilted.

4 Serve each steak on a bed of spinach with the diced courgettes. Drizzle with the remaining basil oil and garnish with basil leaves.

JAPANESE-STYLE SALMON

4tbsp dark soy sauce

4tbsp mirin (a Japanese seasoning, available from supermarkets)

2tbsp sake

2cm (¾in) piece root ginger, cut into slivers, plus extra to garnish

550g (1¼lb) piece of salmon fillet (with skin), cut widthways into four equal pieces

1–2tbsp vegetable oil

serves 2

preparation time: 5 minutes, plus 20 minutes marinating

cooking time: 5 minutes

per serving: 560 cals, 40g fat, nil carbohydrate

You can easily buy ready-made teriyaki sauce, but it's much nicer to make your own, as we've done here. Serve this caramelized salmon with plain boiled rice.

1 Put the soy sauce, mirin, sake and ginger in a shallow bowl and mix together.

2 Add the salmon and leave for 20 minutes.

3 Heat the oil in a non-stick pan until very hot. Fry the fish for 5 minutes or until crisp all over. Garnish with ginger and serve.

RED THAI SEAFOOD CURRY

1 tbsp vegetable oil

3 level tbsp Thai red curry paste

450g (1lb) monkfish tail, boned to make 350g (12oz)
  fillet, sliced into rounds

350g (12oz) large raw, peeled prawns

400ml can half-fat coconut milk

200ml (7fl oz) fish stock

juice of 1 lime

1–2 tbsp Thai fish sauce

125g (4oz) mangetout, sliced lengthways

3 level tbsp torn fresh coriander

serves 4

preparation time: 15 minutes

cooking time: 8–10 minutes

per serving: 350 cals, 19g fat, 5g carbohydrate

Monkfish is lean, has a good meaty flavour and won't fall apart when cooked. Serve with plain boiled rice. *Illustrated.*

1 Heat oil in a large non-stick pan or wok. Add the curry paste and cook for 1–2 minutes.

2 Add the monkfish and prawns and stir well to coat in the curry paste. Add the coconut milk, stock, lime juice and fish sauce. Stir all the ingredients together and bring just to the boil.

3 Add the mangetout and simmer for 5 minutes or until both mangetout and fish are tender. Stir in the coriander and check the seasoning, adding salt and freshly ground black pepper to taste.

tip: *If you can't find half-fat coconut milk, use half a can of full-fat and make up the difference with water or stock. Freeze the remaining milk for up to 1 month.*

SALMON LAKSA

1 tbsp olive oil

2 bunches spring onions, sliced

1 garlic clove, finely chopped

1 large red chilli, deseeded and finely chopped

2.5cm (1in) piece fresh ginger, finely chopped

1–2 level tbsp Thai red curry paste

400ml can coconut milk

300ml (½ pint) fish or vegetable stock

700g (1½lb) skinned salmon fillet, cubed

2 level tbsp chopped fresh coriander

150g (5oz) stir-fry rice noodles

serves 4–6

preparation time: 10 minutes

cooking time: 12 minutes

per serving for 4: 590 cals, 42g fat, 16g carbohydrate

per serving for 6: 390 cals, 28g fat, 10g carbohydrate

If you prefer, you can make the sauce ahead of time, then add the salmon and cook it for a few minutes just before you're ready to eat.

1 Heat the oil in a large frying pan and fry the spring onions, garlic, chilli, ginger and curry paste for 2–3 minutes. Add the coconut milk and stock and bring to the boil.

2 Add the salmon, return to the boil and simmer for 5–6min or until just cooked. Add the coriander and season with salt and freshly ground black pepper.

3 Meanwhile, put the noodles in a bowl with 1 level tsp salt, pour over boiling water to cover and stand for 2 minutes. Drain and put in a large bowl, spoon the salmon and sauce on top and serve.

PAN-ROASTED, SESAME-CRUSTED SALMON

6 × 150g (5oz) pieces cut from salmon fillet, bones
removed (or you could use halibut or line-caught cod)
3 level tbsp sesame seeds or Sanchi Furikake
Japanese seasoning
1 level tbsp Maldon sea salt (or similar good quality
sea salt)
1 tbsp sesame oil
1 tbsp extra-virgin olive oil
50g (2oz) rocket to garnish

serves 6
preparation time: 10 minutes,
plus 20 minutes infusing
cooking time: 5–8 minutes, plus 4 minutes resting
per serving: 360 cals, 26g fat, 1g carbohydrate

A good pan with a tight-fitting lid is essential for this, as the pan becomes an oven – sort of! The lid keeps the fish moist and a meal can be knocked up quite quickly. Depending on the size of your pan, you may only be able to cook four pieces of salmon at once – if so, turn the oven on to keep one batch warm as the other cooks. If you're doing this, cook the fish to medium-rare, then the oven will finish it off. If you cook the salmon with the skin on – it becomes crisp to eat and keeps the moisture in the fish. If you don't like the skin, peel it off before serving. Serve the salmon with the tomatoes and sweet potato mash.

1 Put the pieces of salmon fillet in a plastic tray, skin side down. Put the sesame seeds or Japanese seasoning and the salt in a mortar and grind with a pestle (or use a small spice grinder). Sprinkle the seasoning evenly over each piece of salmon, then cover loosely with clingfilm and leave at room temperature for 20 minutes.

2 Mix the oils together in a small bowl. Turn the salmon over and brush the oil over the skin. Preheat the pan and, when just more than moderately hot, put the salmon in, skin side down. Put the lid on and cook for 5 minutes. Keep an eye on the skin so it doesn't burn – it should be golden brown and crisp.

3 Take the lid off and check the salmon. If the fillets are less than 2cm (¾in) thick, they'll be cooked now (they should still be pink in the middle). If so, turn the heat off, flip the salmon over, then leave to rest for 4 minutes with the lid off. If not, continue to cook for a few minutes with the lid on, then leave to rest, as before. Drizzle the tomato juices over the salmon and garnish with the rocket.

SEARED SALMON WITH LIME DRESSING

4 × 125g (4oz) chunky salmon fillets

4 level tsp seaweed salt (mix together 2 level tsp
 crushed sea salt and 2 level tsp mixed crushed
 peppercorns)

3 limes

2 small fennel bulbs, sliced

2 × 100g packs asparagus tips

150g (5oz) courgettes, washed and cut into batons

1tbsp olive oil

1 red onion, sliced

3tbsp extra-virgin olive oil

serves 4

preparation time: 20 minutes

cooking time: 12 minutes

per serving: 390 cals, 29g fat, 6g carbohydrate

A delicious and speedy supper for any night of the week.

1 Put the salmon fillets in a shallow dish. Sprinkle on the seaweed salt and the grated rind and juice of 1 lime.

2 Heat a non-stick griddle pan until really hot, cook the salmon for 2 minutes on each side to sear, then for a further 2 minutes on each side to cook through.

3 Bring a large pan of salted water to the boil, add the juice of ½ lime, the fennel, asparagus tips and courgettes. Bring to the boil and cook for 3 minutes, then drain.

4 Remove the salmon from the griddle pan and keep warm in a moderate oven. Add the olive oil and red onion to the pan, cook for 1 minute, then squeeze in the juice of ½ lime. Add the fennel, asparagus and courgettes to the pan and stir-fry for a couple of minutes.

5 Whisk together the extra-virgin olive oil and the grated rind and juice of 1 lime. Drizzle the dressing over the salmon and serve with a selection of fresh vegetables.

QUICK FISH AND CHIPS

4 litres (7 pints) sunflower oil

125g (4oz) self-raising flour

¼ level tsp baking powder

¼ level tsp salt

1 medium egg

150ml (¼ pint) sparkling mineral water

2 × 125g (4oz) haddock or hake fillets

450g (1lb) Desirée potatoes, cut into 1cm (½in) chips

serves 2

preparation time: 15 minutes

cooking time: 12 minutes

per serving: 460 cals, 20g fat, 43g carbohydrate

For true 'chip shop' flavour you really do need to deep-fry fish and chips, but this is time consuming. Tradition dictates that chips should be cooked at a higher temperature than the fish, but we've found that cooking a portion of chips and fish at the same time in the deep-fryer works well and it means you can cook to order.

1 Pour the oil into a deep-fat fryer and heat it to 190°C or until a 2.5cm (1in) cube of bread browns in 60 seconds.

2 Put the flour, baking powder, salt, egg and water in a processor and blend to combine. (Or put the ingredients in a bowl and beat everything together until smooth.) Remove the blade and drop one fillet into the batter to coat it.

3 Put half the chips in the deep-fat fryer, then add the battered fish. Fry for 6 minutes until just cooked, then remove and drain well on kitchen paper. Keep warm if not serving immediately.

4 Drop the remaining fillet into the batter to coat, then repeat step 3 with the remaining chips. Serve both portions with salt, vinegar and garlic mayonnaise.

ARBROATH SMOKIES

1 Arbroath Smoky, or smoked haddock, approx 250g
25g (1oz) butter, softened, plus extra to butter foil

serves 1–2
preparation time: 5 minutes
cooking time: 15 minutes
per serving for 1: 440 cals, 23g fat, nil carbohydrate
per serving for 2: 220 cals, 11g fat, nil carbohydrate

This smoked haddock (or whiting) is already cooked so can be served hot or cold. It's very good buttered and warmed through in the oven with bread. If you fancy making more of a meal of it, serve it with parsley mash and a poached egg. *Illustrated.*

1 Preheat the oven to 200°C (180°C fan oven) mark 6. Put the fish on a board and carefully open it up – don't worry if the fish breaks up slightly. Ease out the backbone from the top of the fish, pull it out carefully then discard. Keep the fish open.
2 Season the fish with a little salt and plenty of freshly ground black pepper, then spread butter over one of the fillets. Put the fish halves back together, season the outside, then wrap it in a piece of buttered foil. Put in the oven and cook for 10–15 minutes until the butter has melted and the fish is hot. Serve with bread and butter.

JAPANESE CRAB SALAD

300g (11oz) courgettes
300g (11oz) carrots
1tbsp rice wine vinegar
3tbsp mirin or sweet sherry
2 dressed crab, 175g (6oz) each
1–2 level tsp Japanese pickled ginger,
   sliced or chopped
⅛ level tsp wasabi paste, plus a little to garnish
picked ginger to garnish

serves 4
preparation time: 20 minutes, plus 10 minutes chilling
per serving: 120 cals, 1g fat, 7g carbohydrate

This is a delicious and healthy recipe that tastes as good as it looks.

1 Using a wide vegetable peeler, cut the courgettes and carrots into thin ribbons, put in a bowl of iced water and chill for 15 minutes.
2 Drain and dry the ribbons very well, put in a large bowl, add the vinegar and 2tbsp of the mirin, and season with salt and freshly ground black pepper. Divide between four plates.
3 Pick over the crab meat and remove any remnants of shell, then put the crab meat in a bowl. Add the pickled ginger, wasabi paste and remaining mirin. Season with salt and pepper.
4 Spoon the crab meat on top of the vegetable ribbons, garnish with the picked ginger and a little – make sure it's a little! – wasabi. Serve chilled.

THAI-STYLE TIGER PRAWNS WITH PAK CHOI

3 level tbsp red Thai curry paste

200ml (7fl oz) coconut milk

juice of 1 lime

24 raw tiger prawns, de-veined, shelled with tail on

8 fresh kaffir lime leaves

4 long lemongrass stalks, outer layer removed

2 × 200g packs pak choi, cut in half lengthways

1tbsp light soy sauce

2 level tbsp sweet chilli sauce

serves 4

preparation time: 10 minutes,
    plus 15 minutes marinating

cooking time: 5 minutes

per serving: 168 cals, 8g fat, 8g carbohydrate

These shellfish are marinated in a ready-made paste and coconut milk, then grilled on lemongrass skewers, subtly infusing the prawns with extra flavour.

1 Put the curry paste in a bowl. Add the coconut milk, half the lime juice and the prawns. Stir to coat, cover and chill for 15 minutes. Preheat the grill.

2 Carefully skewer six prawns and two lime leaves on to each lemongrass stalk. Cook under the grill for 5 minutes or until the prawns are pink and cooked through.

3 Meanwhile, put the pak choi in a steamer over a pan of boiling water, cover and cook for 3–4 minutes.

4 Toss the pak choi in the soy sauce and remaining lime juice and season. Serve with the prawn skewers, drizzled with sweet chilli sauce.

VEGETARIAN SUPPERS

This style of eating has become so popular that the idea of a main meal without meat or fish is not unusual. People are more aware of the delicious possibilities and vegetarian food is no longer a specialized taste. Vegetarian dishes are recognized as healthy options, more likely to be low in fat and high in fibre. Another bonus is that, for much the same effort, you can produce a fine meal that is far lower in cost. This collection of recipes has been inspired by cuisine from around the world – from the European elegance of French roulade and a satisfying Italian gnocchi, to the rich spicy stew of the Moroccan souk.

CARROT ROULADE WITH WATERCRESS FILLING

2 level tbsp freshly grated Parmesan cheese

1 level tbsp chopped fresh coriander,
  plus 12 extra whole leaves

125g (4oz) butter

700g (1½lb) carrots, finely grated

6 medium eggs, separated

for the watercress filling

6 medium eggs, hard-boiled and shelled

1 bunch of watercress, stalks removed

200g (7oz) good-quality mayonnaise

serves 6

preparation time: 15 minutes, plus chilling

cooking time: 20 minutes

per serving: 640 cals, 59g fat, 9g carbohydrate

Watercress and egg mayonnaise combine to create a creamy filling wrapped in a savoury carrot sponge. *Illustrated.*

1 Line a 33 × 23cm (13 × 9in) Swiss roll tin with baking parchment. Sprinkle the Parmesan over the paper, then scatter the whole coriander leaves on top.

2 Melt the butter in a frying pan. Add the carrots and cook gently for 10 minutes or until soft. Drain well, tip into a bowl and beat in the egg yolks. Season well.

3 Whisk the egg whites in a clean bowl until stiff, then fold into the mixture with the chopped coriander. Spoon into the prepared tin and spread evenly. Bake at 200°C (180°C fan oven) mark 6 for 10–12 minutes or until golden brown and springy to the touch.

4 For the filling, chop the eggs, and finely chop the watercress. Put both in a bowl with the mayonnaise and mix well, seasoning with salt and pepper to taste.

5 Turn the roulade out on to a sheet of greaseproof paper and spread with the filling, leaving a 1cm (½in) border. Beginning from a short side and using the greaseproof paper to help, roll up. Trim the edges to neaten. Chill until ready to serve, then cut into slices.

DELI PIZZA

6 level tbsp tomato pizza sauce

2 pizzeria-style pizza bases

100g (3½oz) soft goat's cheese

1 red onion, finely sliced

100g (3½oz) sunblush tomatoes

100g (3½oz) olives

Handful of fresh basil, roughly torn

serves 4

preparation time: 5 minutes

cooking time: 15 minutes

per serving: 370 cals, 10g fat, 57g carbohydrate

There are some excellent ready-made pizzas available nowadays – this one is par-cooked, so it just needs finishing off. Top with a smear of tomato sauce, some creamy goat's cheese and a few bits from the supermarket deli counter – we've used sunblush tomatoes and a selection of olives, but marinated artichokes, peppers or chargrilled aubergines would work just as well.

1 Put a large baking sheet on the top shelf of the oven and preheat to 220°C (200°C fan oven) mark 7.

2 To make the pizza topping, spread a thin layer of the tomato sauce over the ready-made bases. Top with dollops of goat's cheese, then scatter over the red onion, tomatoes and olives.

3 Bake on the preheated baking sheet for 15 minutes or until golden and crispy. Scatter over the torn basil and serve immediately with a crisp green salad.

HALLOUMI WITH SPICY COUSCOUS

300g (11oz) couscous

600ml (1 pint) hot vegetable stock

270g jar roasted red peppers

1 level tsp chilli flakes

grated zest and juice of 1 lemon

2 × 250g packs of halloumi cheese,
  cut into thick slices

2 level tbsp chopped fresh mint

serves 4

preparation time: 5 minutes

cooking time: 8–12 minutes

per serving: 860 cals, 50g fat, 58g carbohydrate

This waxy cheese is perfect for frying as it holds its shape well.

1 Put the couscous in a bowl and pour over the hot vegetable stock. Cover and leave to sit for 5–10 minutes.

2 Meanwhile, put 6tbsp of oil reserved from the peppers in a bowl and add the chilli flakes, lemon zest and juice. Add the halloumi and mix together to coat. Set aside.

3 Heat a large frying pan over a medium heat. Fry the cheese slices in batches, spaced well apart, for 2 minutes on each side until golden. Cover and keep warm.

4 Use a fork to fluff up the couscous, then add the peppers, mint and any remaining oil from the halloumi marinade. Toss well and serve with the cheese.

CREAMY GARLIC MUSHROOMS

2tbsp olive oil

1 onion, finely sliced

2 garlic cloves, crushed

450g (1lb) button mushrooms

75ml (3fl oz) white wine

100ml (3½fl oz) crème fraîche

4 level tbsp chopped fresh chives

serves 4

preparation time: 3 minutes

cooking time: 17 minutes

per serving: 190 cals, 17g fat, 5g carbohydrate

The earthy flavour of mushrooms is the hero here. Just add melting onion, crème fraîche and chives for an indulgent vegetarian dinner.

1 Heat the oil in a pan and fry the onion for 10 minutes over a medium heat until golden, stirring from time to time to make sure it doesn't burn.

2 Add the garlic and cook for 1 minute. Add the mushrooms and toss lightly, then cover and cook for 2 minutes.

3 Add the white wine and crème fraîche, season well with salt and freshly ground black pepper, and stir everything together. Cover, bring up to the boil and bubble for about 4 minutes or until the mushrooms are tender, then stir in the chives. Serve with rice or on toasted brioche.

MUSHROOMS 'EN CROÛTE'

2 garlic cloves, crushed

5 sun-dried tomatoes, roughly chopped

4 black olives in brine, drained, pitted
and roughly chopped

pinch of crushed dried chillies

dash of teriyaki or soy sauce

250ml (9fl oz) vegetable stock

125ml (4fl oz) red wine

700g (1½lb) button mushrooms

ciabatta bread, sliced

chopped flat-leafed parsley and
crushed black pepper to garnish

serves 4–6

preparation time: 5 minutes

cooking time: 15 minutes

per serving for 4: 250 cals , 5g fat, 43g carbohydrate

per serving for 6: 230 cals , 4g fat, 42g carbohydrate
(assumes 2 slices of bread per serving)

Serve with a salad of bitter leaves, such as radicchio, chicory and curly endive.

1 Combine the garlic, sun-dried tomatoes, olives, chillies, teriyaki or soy sauce, 175ml (6fl oz) of the stock and all the wine in a large frying pan. Simmer briskly until the liquid has reduced to about 1tbsp.

2 Add the mushrooms and remaining stock. Simmer for 8–10 minutes, stirring occasionally, until the mushrooms are bathed in a syrupy sauce and tender, but not too soft.

3 Preheat the grill. Lightly toast the ciabatta on both sides until golden. Arrange the ciabatta slices on individual heatproof serving dishes. Ladle a generous amount of mushrooms on to each, garnish with the parsley and black pepper and serve at once.

TOMATO CROSTINI WITH FETA AND BASIL DRESSING

1 small garlic clove, crushed

3 level tbsp chopped fresh basil

25g (1oz) pinenuts

2tbsp extra-virgin olive oil

grated zest and juice of 1 lime

50g (2oz) feta cheese

4 large tomatoes, preferably vine ripened, thickly sliced

150g tub fresh tomato salsa

50g (2oz) pitted black olives, roughly chopped

4 thick slices country-style bread

basil leaves to garnish

serves 2–4

preparation time: 20 minutes

per serving for 2: 570 cals, 33g fat, 56g carbohydrate

per serving for 4: 290 cals , 16g fat, 28g carbohydrate

Perfect for a light summer supper, this Mediterranean open sandwich is a meal in itself.

1 Whiz the garlic, basil, pinenuts, olive oil, lime rind and juice together in a food processor to form a smooth paste. Add the cheese and blend. Thin with 1tbsp water if necessary. Season.

2 Put the tomatoes, salsa and olives in a bowl and toss together. Divide the tomato mixture between the slices of bread and spoon the basil dressing over the top. Garnish with basil leaves and serve.

ROASTED MEDITERRANEAN VEGETABLES

8 large plum tomatoes, halved

2 large red peppers, deseeded and each cut into eight

2 large garlic cloves, crushed

50g (2oz) pinenuts

1tbsp balsamic vinegar

3 level tbsp capers

handful fresh thyme leaves

serves 4

preparation time: 5 minutes

cooking time: 15 minutes

per serving: 160 cals, 12g fat , 8g carbohydrate

Peppers, tomatoes and pinenuts are tossed in oil and garlic, and fast-roasted until tender – then sprinkled with capers and thyme to serve.

1 Preheat the oven to 220°C (200°C fan oven) mark 7. Put the tomatoes in a roasting tin with the peppers, garlic and pine nuts. Season with freshly ground black pepper and roast for 15 minutes.

2 Add the balsamic vinegar, capers and thyme to the roasting tin. Mix gently to combine and serve with a salad and plenty of crusty bread to mop up the juices.

SPICED BEAN AND VEGETABLE STEW

3tbsp olive oil

2 small onions, sliced

2 garlic cloves, crushed

1 level tbsp sweet paprika

1 small dried red chilli, deseeded and finely chopped

700g (1½lb) sweet potatoes, peeled and cubed

700g (1½lb) pumpkin, peeled and cut into chunks

125g (4oz) okra, trimmed

500g passata

400g can haricot or cannellini beans, drained

serves 6

preparation time: 5 minutes

cooking time: 25 minutes

per serving: 250 cals, 8g fat, 42g carbohydrate

A satisfying stew with paprika and chilli to spice up an autumn evening.

1 Heat the oil in a large heavy-based pan, add the onions and garlic and cook over a very gentle heat for 5 minutes. Stir in the paprika and chilli and cook for 2 minutes.

2 Add the sweet potatoes, pumpkin, okra, passata and 900ml (1½ pints) water. Season generously with salt and freshly ground black pepper. Cover, bring to the boil and simmer for 20 minutes until the vegetables are tender. Add the beans and cook for 3 minutes to warm through.

ROASTED VEG AND ROCKET TARTLETS

375g pack ready-rolled puff pastry

a little plain flour for rolling out

1 medium egg, beaten

2 level tbsp coarse sea salt

300g (11oz) vegetable antipasti in oil (mixed
   roasted peppers, artichokes, onions etc)
   from your local deli counter

a little olive oil, if needed

2tbsp balsamic vinegar

190g tub red pepper hummus

50g bag wild rocket

serves 6

preparation time: 10 minutes

cooking time: 5–7 minutes

per serving: 340 cals, 23g fat, 27g carbohydrate

This recipe is incredibly easy to make and can be prepared in advance, requiring just a bit of last-minute assembly. Squares of puff pastry are cooked until golden brown, then topped with the best ingredients from the deli counter. Here, we've used red pepper hummus and roasted vegetables with peppery rocket tossed in a sweet balsamic dressing.

1 Preheat the oven to 220°C (200°C fan oven) mark 7. Unroll the puff pastry on a lightly floured surface and cut it into six equal sized squares

2 Put pastry squares on a large baking sheet and prick each one all over with a fork. Brush all over with beaten egg and sprinkle the edges with sea salt. Bake for 5–7 minutes or until the pastry is golden brown and cooked through.

3 Pour off 4tbsp olive oil from the antipasti (you may need to add a little extra olive oil) into a bowl. Add the balsamic vinegar. Season well, then set aside.

4 To serve, divide the hummus among the pastry bases, spreading it over each. Put each on an individual plate and spoon over the antipasti – there's no need to be neat.

5 Whisk the balsamic vinegar dressing together. Add the rocket leaves and toss to coat, then pile a small handful of leaves on top of each tartlet. Serve immediately.

VEGETABLE AND CHICKPEA COUSCOUS

350g (12oz) each onions, carrots, fennel and
   courgettes, cut into large chunks
1.1 litres (2 pints) vegetable stock
2 bay leaves
1 large red pepper, cut into large chunks
400g can chickpeas, drained
350g (12oz) couscous
25g (1oz) butter
1 level tsp salt

serves 6
preparation time: 10 minutes
cooking time: 20 minutes
per serving: 360 cals, 6g fat, 61g carbohydrate

Couscous has a wonderful soft grainy texture with a sweet flavour and the beauty of it is that it involves very little cooking and can be ready in moments. Traditionally, it's steamed in a couscoussier, but with today's quick-cook couscous all you need is a deep pan or bowl. If you want your vegetables hot and spicy just add a little harissa – a very spicy sauce made with hot chilli peppers, garlic and olive oil – which is increasingly available in supermarkets.

1 Put the onions, carrots and fennel in a large pan with the vegetable stock and bay leaves and season well with salt and pepper. Bring slowly to the boil and cook for 5–10 minutes or until the vegetables begin to soften.
2 Take off the heat, add the courgettes, red pepper and chickpeas, return to the boil and cook for 3–4 minutes.
3 Meanwhile, soak the couscous according to packet instructions with 1 level tsp salt. Melt the butter in a large, deep frying pan. Add the couscous, break up the grains with a fork, heat through and season. Add the hot vegetables to the couscous and serve.

TOMATO TARTS WITH FETA CHEESE

150g (5oz) sheet ready-rolled puff pastry

300g (11oz) plum tomatoes, thinly sliced

pinch of caster sugar

150g (5oz) feta cheese, crumbled

1 level tbsp chopped fresh thyme

1tbsp extra-virgin olive oil

serves 4

preparation time: 10 minutes

cooking time: 15–20 minutes

per serving: 250 cals, 18g fat, 15g carbohydrate

If you have time, it's a good idea to sprinkle the sliced tomatoes with a little salt and leave for 30 minutes to draw out some of the juice before draining and using them, as the pastry will then be crisper. These tarts can be served hot or cold and are ideal for a picnic.

1 Preheat the oven. Cut the puff pastry into four rectangles. Arrange the tomatoes on top, sprinkle over the caster sugar and season well with salt and freshly ground black pepper. Sprinkle the feta and thyme on top and drizzle with the olive oil.

2 Bake the tarts at 200°C (180°C fan oven) mark 6 for 15–20 minutes or until the pastry is golden brown and risen.

EGGS AND CHEESE

Eggs must be the ultimate fast food, not only do they take minutes to cook, they are good for you and are full of protein, vitamins and minerals as well as being low calorie. Whether it is for a solo snack or a family meal, the humble egg can offer many choices.

When it comes to cheese, we really are spoilt for choice. It truly is the most magical foodstuff. Such a simple ingredient doesn't need to be messed about with, and you can see from these recipes how quickly it can make a satisfying meal. You can mix and match your cheeses with salads, vegetables and different breads in a choice of hot or cold dishes, to suit your mood and appetite.

COURGETTE AND PARMESAN FRITTATA

40g (1½oz) butter

1 small onion, finely chopped

225g (8oz) courgettes, trimmed and finely sliced

6 medium eggs, beaten

25g (1oz) freshly grated Parmesan cheese, plus
   shavings to garnish

serves 4

preparation time: 10 minutes

cooking time: 12 minutes

per serving: 260 cals, 20g fat, 4g carbohydrate

variation cherry tomato and rocket frittata: *Replace the
courgettes with 175g (6oz) vine-ripened cherry tomatoes, frying
them for 1 minute only, until they begin to soften. Immediately
after pouring in the eggs, scatter 25g (1oz) rocket leaves over
the surface. Continue as above.*

**A posh Italian omelette: this delicious frittata can be made
in minutes. *Illustrated.***

1 Melt 25g (1oz) of the butter in an 18cm (7 in) non-stick frying
pan and cook the onion for about 10 minutes until softened. Add
the courgettes and fry gently for 5 minutes or until they begin
to soften.

2 Meanwhile, beat the eggs in a bowl and season well with
salt and freshly ground black pepper. Add the remaining butter
to the pan and heat, then pour in the eggs. Cook for 2–3 minutes
or until golden underneath and cooked around the edges.

3 Sprinkle the grated cheese over the frittata and grill
under a medium-high heat for 1–2 minutes or until just set.
Scatter with Parmesan shavings, cut into quarters and serve
with crusty bread.

GOAT'S CHEESE AND RED ONION CROSTINI

1 large red onion

2 tbsp olive oil, plus extra to drizzle

75g (3oz) soft goat's cheese

Slices of sourdough or ciabatta bread
   (allow three per person)

chopped fresh thyme to garnish

makes 8 crostini

preparation time: 20 minutes

cooking time: 5 minutes

per serving: 190 cals, 8g fat, 25g carbohydrate

**For a light supper, it's easy to make perfect crostini. Serve
them with this topping, a bowl of black olives and a glass
of chilled Sauvignon Blanc.**

1 To make the crostini, toast the slices of bread, brush with
olive oil and rub with a garlic clove.

2 For the topping, put the onion on a baking sheet, drizzle with
2 tbsp of the olive oil and grill for 5 minutes or until soft and just
beginning to char.

3 Spread the goat's cheese on each crostini; top with the onion
and some freshly ground black pepper. Drizzle with oil and
garnish with thyme to serve.

CRUSHED POTATOES WITH FETA AND OLIVES

700g (1½lb) new potatoes, unpeeled

75ml (3fl oz) olive oil

75g (3oz) pitted black olives, shredded

2 level tbsp chopped flat-leafed parsley

200g (7oz) feta cheese, crumbled

serves 4

preparation time: 15 minutes

cooking time: 15 minutes

per serving: 420 cals, 30g fat, 29g carbohydrate

The saltiness of the feta works well with the new potatoes.
Illustrated.

Cook the potatoes (in their skins) in a pan of boiling salted water for 15 minutes or until tender. Drain, return to the pan and crush roughly. Add the olive oil, olives, flat-leafed parsley and feta cheese. Season and toss together – don't overmix or the potatoes will become glutinous.

HALLOUMI AND AVOCADO SALAD

3tbsp lemon juice

8tbsp olive oil

3 level tbsp chopped fresh mint

250g pack halloumi, sliced into eight

1 level tbsp flour, seasoned

2tbsp oil

200g bag mixed leaf salad

2 avocados, stoned, peeled and sliced

flat-leafed parsley to garnish

serves 4

preparation time: 10 minutes

cooking time: 2 minutes

per serving: 710 cals, 69g fat, 5g carbohyrate

Halloumi is a Greek cheese ideal for frying or grilling, but best cooked just before serving.

1 To make the dressing, whisk the lemon juice together with the olive oil and mint, then season with salt and freshly ground black pepper.

2 Coat the halloumi with the flour. Heat the oil in a large frying pan and fry the cheese for 1 minute on each side or until it forms a golden crust.

3 Meanwhile, in a large bowl, add half the dressing to the salad leaves and avocado and toss together. Arrange the hot cheese on top and drizzle over the remaining dressing. Garnish with the parsley and serve.

POTATO AND CHORIZO TORTILLA

6tbsp olive oil

450g (1lb) potatoes, very thinly sliced

225g (8oz) onions, thinly sliced

2 garlic cloves, finely chopped

50g (2oz) sliced chorizo, cut into thin strips

6 large eggs, lightly beaten

serves 4

preparation time: 5 minutes

cooking time: 25 minutes

per serving: 450cals, 33g fat, 23g carbophydrate

This thick Spanish omelette can also be eaten cold – ideal for a picnic, or cut into strips and served with drinks.

1 Heat the oil in a non-stick frying pan, measuring about 18cm (7in) across the base. Add the potatoes, onions and garlic. Stir together until coated in the oil, then cover the pan. Cook gently, stirring from time to time, for 10–15 minutes or until the potato is soft. Season with salt.

2 Add the chorizo to the potato mixture. Season the eggs with salt and freshly ground black pepper and pour on to the potato mixture. Cook over a moderate heat for 5 minutes or until beginning to brown at the edges and the egg is about three-quarters set. Put the pan under a preheated grill to brown the top. The egg should be a little soft in the middle as it continues to cook and set as it cools.

3 Carefully loosen the tortilla round the edge and underneath with a flexible turner, cut into wedges and serve.

MUSHROOM AND SAGE FRITTATA

2tbsp olive oil

2 large onions, finely sliced

150g (5oz) baby chestnut mushrooms, sliced

75g (3oz) pecorino cheese, coarsely grated

6 sage leaves, roughly chopped, plus extra to garnish

6 large organic eggs, beaten

serves 4

preparation time: 5 minutes, plus 3 minutes standing

cooking time: 25–30 minutes

per serving: 244 cals, 23g fat, 6g carbohydrate

Cooking the frittata in the oven ensures an even set all round. *Illustrated.*

1 Preheat the oven to 200°C (180°C fan oven) mark 6. Line an 18 × 28 × 2.5cm (7 × 11 × 1in) tin with baking parchment.

2 Heat the oil in a pan and fry the onions gently for 10–15 minutes or until soft. Increase the heat, add the mushrooms and cook for 2 minutes, then tip into the prepared tin. Sprinkle over the cheese and chopped sage leaves.

3 Season the eggs well, then pour into the tin. Cook in the oven for 15–20 minutes until just firm in the centre and lightly golden. Leave to stand for 2–3 minutes.

4 Loosen the frittata around the edges, turn out on to a chopping board and cut into four wedges. Serve garnished with the remaining sage.

SUPPER OMELETTE

225g (8oz) piece of salami, chorizo or garlic sausage,
  roughly chopped

50g (2oz) stale baguette or garlic bread,
  roughly chopped

8 large eggs

2 spring onions, finely chopped

1 small bunch chives, or any other fresh herbs
  you fancy, finely chopped

1tbsp olive oil

serves 4

preparation time: 5 minutes

cooking time: 15 minutes

per serving: 520 cals, 42g fat, 7g carbohydrate

A Spanish-style omelette is a good way to use up the odds and ends in the fridge.

1 Heat a large 28cm (11in) frying pan and fry the salami or chorizo pieces over a gentle heat until the fat begins to run. Increase the heat and cook the meat until golden and crisp. Remove from the pan (leaving the fat in the pan) and set aside.

2 Add the bread to the pan and fry until it's also golden and crisp. Remove the pan from the heat, mix the croutons with the cooked salami and keep warm until needed.

3 Beat the eggs together with the spring onions and chives, then season well.

4 Heat the oil in the pan used for the salami and bread. When very hot, add the egg mixture, allowing the liquid to spread across the base of the pan. Cook for 2 minutes, then draw the cooked edges into the centre with a spatula, tilting the pan so the runny mixture runs into the gap.

5 When the omelette is almost set, turn the heat down and spoon the salami and crouton mixture evenly over the top. Cook for a further 30 seconds, then cut the omelette into four wedges. Serve with a soft, leafy salad and some crusty bread.

ROQUEFORT AND REDCURRANT SALAD

1½tbsp redcurrant jelly

1tbsp white wine vinegar

pinch English mustard powder

4tbsp extra-virgin olive oil

a selection of bitter leaves such as curly endive,
    radicchio and chicory

225g (8oz) Roquefort cheese, crumbled

125g (4oz) punnet fresh redcurrants – reserve four
    sprays to garnish and destalk the rest

serves 4

preparation time: 10 minutes

per serving: 360 cals, 32g fat, 6g carbohydrate

This colourful salad is a magic sweet-savoury combination.
Illustrated.

1 In a small bowl, whisk together the redcurrant jelly, 1tsp boiling water, the vinegar, mustard powder and oil. Season with salt and freshly ground black pepper.

2 Arrange the mixed salad leaves and Roquefort on a large plate. Spoon the dressing over the top and sprinkle with the redcurrants. Garnish with redcurrant sprays and serve immediately.

PIPERADE

2tbsp olive oil

1 medium onion, finely chopped

1 garlic clove, finely chopped

1 red pepper, deseeded and chopped

375g (13oz) tomatoes, peeled, deseeded and chopped

pinch of cayenne pepper

8 large eggs

chopped flat-leafed parsley to garnish

serves 4

preparation time: 5 minutes

cooking time: 25 minutes

per serving: 280 cals, 20g fat, 8g carbohydrate

When cooled, this classic French recipe makes a delicious sandwich filling in a hollowed-out crisp French baguette.

1 Heat the oil in a heavy-based frying pan, add the onion and garlic and cook gently for 5 minutes. Add the red pepper and cook for 10 minutes or until softened.

2 Add the tomatoes, raise the heat and cook until they're reduced to a thick pulp. Season well with cayenne pepper, salt and freshly ground black pepper.

3 Lightly whisk the eggs and add to the frying pan. Using a wooden spoon, stir gently until they've just begun to set but are still creamy. Garnish with parsley and serve immediately.

MUSHROOM SOUFFLÉ OMELETTE

50g (2oz) small chestnut mushrooms, wiped and sliced

3 level tbsp crème fraîche

2 medium eggs, separated

15g (½oz) butter

5 chives, roughly chopped

serves 1

preparation time: 5 minutes

cooking time: 7 minutes

per serving: 480 cals, 44g fat, 1g carbohydrate

Anything with the word soufflé in it sounds complicated, but don't be put off – this delicious recipe is an unashamedly simple meal for one. *Illustrated.*

1 Heat a small non-stick frying pan for 30 seconds. Add mushrooms, cook for 3 minutes, stirring to brown slightly, then stir in the crème fraîche and turn off the heat.

2 Lightly beat the egg yolks, add 2tbsp cold water and season with salt and freshly ground black pepper.

3 In a separate bowl, whisk the egg whites until stiff but not dry, then gently fold into the egg yolks. Be careful not to overmix them.

4 Preheat a grill. Heat an 18cm (7in) non-stick frying pan and melt the butter in it. Add the egg mixture, tilting the pan in all directions to cover the base. Cook over a medium heat for 3 minutes or until the underside is golden brown.

5 Gently reheat the mushrooms and add the chives. Put the omelette under the grill for 1 minute, or until the surface is just firm and puffy. Pour on the mushrooms. Run a spatula gently round and underneath the omelette to loosen it, then carefully fold it and turn on to a plate.

ARTICHOKE AND GOAT'S CHEESE TOASTS

225g jar artichoke antipasto, drained and oil reserved

225g (8oz) firm goat's cheese, such as Crottin, rind removed and diced

1 level tbsp chopped fresh thyme

grated rind of 1 lemon and 1tbsp lemon juice

½ level tsp grainy mustard

4 thick slices flavoured bread, such as olive or rosemary, toasted

70g pack cured Serrano or Parma ham

olive oil to drizzle

thyme sprigs and crushed black pepper to garnish

serves 4

preparation time: 15 minutes

per serving: 410 cals, 24g fat, 26g carbohydrate

Cheese on toast has never tasted this good.

1 Halve the artichokes and put in a large bowl with the goat's cheese and chopped fresh thyme.

2 Whisk the lemon zest and juice with salt, freshly ground black pepper, the mustard and 3tbsp of the reserved oil, then stir into the artichoke mixture.

3 Divide the mixture between the slices of toast and arrange the ham on top. Drizzle with olive oil, garnish with thyme sprigs and crushed black pepper and serve immediately.

GOAT'S CHEESE AND WALNUT SALAD

2tbsp red wine vinegar

8tbsp olive oil

large pinch of caster sugar

1 large radicchio, shredded

2 bunches prepared watercress,
 about 125g (4oz) total weight

1 red onion, finely sliced

150g (5oz) walnut pieces

2 x 100g packs goat's cheese, crumbled

serves 4

preparation time: 10 minutes

per serving: 620 cals, 58g fat, 6g carbohydrate

We recommend an organic Welsh goat's cheese for this recipe. It has a lovely mild flavour and is easy to crumble. *Illustrated.*

1 To make the salad dressing, mix the vinegar, olive oil, caster sugar, salt and freshly ground black pepper thoroughly. Put to one side.

2 Put the radicchio, watercress and onion in a large bowl. Pour over the dressing and toss well.

3 Sprinkle over the walnuts and goat's cheese. Serve with French bread.

ANTIPASTI SALAD

juice of 1 lime

4 ripe pears, peaches or nectarines, halved,
 stoned and sliced

50g (2oz) rocket leaves

4–5 small firm round goat's cheeses, thickly sliced

4 grilled red peppers, sliced, or a 285g jar pimientos,
 drained

2 small red onions, sliced into petals

handful of black olives

olive oil to drizzle

serves 6

preparation time: 20 min

per serving: 170 cals, 9g fat, 17g carbohydrate

You can make up your own combination for this wonderful mixed salad platter according to what's available and in season.

1 Squeeze the lime juice over the fruit and add a sprinkling of freshly ground black pepper.

2 Starting in the centre with the rocket, arrange all the ingredients in lines on a large serving plate.

3 Cover with clingfilm and keep in a cool place. Use within 2 hours. Drizzle with olive oil just before serving.

EGGS BENEDICT

200g jar hollandaise sauce

1tbsp malt vinegar

4 very fresh medium eggs, preferably organic

4 slices cooked ham

4 English muffins, split and toasted

serves 4

preparation time: 10 minutes

cooking time: 12 minutes

per serving: 580 cals, 52g fat, 26g carbohydrate

This recipe, which is originally American, is a favourite choice for brunch, although it is filling enough to make a light supper. Hollandaise sauce transforms a plain poached egg into something deliciously rich.

1 Stand the jar of hollandaise sauce in a deep narrow heatproof bowl, pour around boiling water to almost immerse the jar and leave to warm while you cook the eggs.

2 Fill a wide, shallow pan two-thirds full with boiling water and add the vinegar. Carefully break an egg into a saucer. Using a large spoon, make a whirlpool in the boiling water and lower the egg into the water. Reduce the heat and cook gently for 3 minutes or until the white is just set and the yolk soft.

3 Lift the egg out of the pan with a draining spoon and put in a shallow dish of warm water. Repeat the process with the remaining eggs.

4 Warm the ham in the microwave for 1 minute on Medium. On each plate put a toasted muffin half, carefully add a poached egg, top with a slice of ham, a couple of large spoonfuls of warm hollandaise sauce and the other half of the muffin. Repeat the process with the remaining muffins, eggs, ham and hollandaise sauce. Serve at once.

SIDE DISHES

These are dishes that will be used again and again, so they are designed to be very quick and easy. You can see instantly how much butter is needed for garlic bread and how to achieve a perfectly fluffy couscous. Colcannon is a huge favourite and a regular feature in a cook's repertoire. It is great to see mashed potato making a big comeback, even in posh restaurants, and this Irish version flavoured with cabbage is a very appealing and comforting dish.

TURKISH TOMATOES

36 on-the-vine cherry tomatoes, picked from the stem

3tbsp extra-virgin olive oil

1 level tsp Maldon sea salt

½ tsp dried chilli flakes (make sure they're fresh)

juice of 1 small lemon

3 level tbsp freshly chopped dill

serves 6

preparation time: 5 minutes, plus 10 minutes infusing

cooking time: 5 minutes

per serving: 70 cals, 7g fat, 2g carbohydrate

A delicious and simple dish which works well with fish or pasta. *Illustrated.*

1 Heat the pan and, when moderately hot, add the tomatoes, 1tbsp of the olive oil and the salt. Cook, shaking the pan, until the tomatoes begin to colour and the skins of around six of them have burst.

2 Add the chilli flakes and lemon juice and shake for a few seconds. Add the remaining oil, count to 20, then take off the heat.

3 Tip into a bowl and cool for 10 minutes. Stir in the dill, cover with clingfilm and put to one side for around 10 minutes so the flavours can mature.

GRIDDLED GARLIC BREAD

1 large crusty loaf

175g (6oz) butter, cubed

3 garlic cloves, crushed

a bunch of stiff-stemmed fresh thyme sprigs

serves 8

preparation time: 5 minutes

cooking time: 5–6 minutes

per serving: 400 cals, 20g fat, 49g carbohydrate

Everyone loves garlic bread, and it makes any meal more delicious and filling.

1 Cut the bread into 2cm (¾in) slices.

2 Melt the butter with the garlic in a small pan. Or, put the butter and garlic in a small metal or heatproof dish (a tin mug is ideal) and sit it on the barbecue grill. Leave to melt. Season with salt and freshly ground black pepper.

3 Dip the thyme into the melted butter and brush one side of each slice of bread. Put the slices, buttered side down, on the barbecue grill. Cook for 1–2 minutes until crisp and golden. Brush uppermost sides with the remaining butter; turn over and cook. Or, preheat a griddle pan and cook the garlic bread as on the barbecue. Serve hot.

COLCANNON

900g (2lb) potatoes, cut into even-sized chunks

50g (2oz) butter

¼ Savoy cabbage, shredded

100ml (3½fl oz) semi-skimmed milk

serves 4

preparation time: 10 minutes

cooking time: 20 minutes

per serving: 310 cals, 12g fat, 45g carbohydrate

That's the Irish name for this dish – sautéed Savoy cabbage mixed into soft, fluffy mashed potato.

1 Put the potatoes in a pan and cover with cold water. Put a lid on the pan and bring up to the boil. Simmer, half-covered, for 15–20 minutes or until the potatoes are tender.

2 Meanwhile, melt the butter in a frying pan, and stir-fry the cabbage for 3 minutes.

3 Drain the potatoes well, then tip back in the pan and put over a medium heat for 1–2 minutes to drive off the steam. Tip in the colander and cover to keep warm.

4 Put the milk in the potato pan. Bring to the boil, add the potatoes and mash. Add the cabbage and any butter from the pan and mix. Season and serve immediately.

SAFFRON RICE

500g (1lb 2oz) basmati rice

900ml (1½ pints) stock made with 1½ chicken
   stock cubes

5tbsp sunflower or light vegetable oil

½ level tsp saffron

75g (3oz) blanched almonds and pistachio nuts,
   coarsely chopped, to garnish (optional)

serves 8

preparation time: 5–10 minutes

cooking time: 25 minutes

per serving: 350 cals, 13g fat, 50g carbohydrate

In some Oriental communities, grains of rice are a symbol of abundance and fecundity, while the colour yellow is seen as celebratory and is thought to evoke happiness. *Illustrated.*

1 To clean the rice, put it in a bowl and cover with warm water, then drain well through a sieve.

2 Put the chicken stock, oil and a good pinch of salt in a pan, then cover it and bring to the boil. Add the saffron and the rice.

3 Cover the pan and bring the stock to the boil, then stir and turn the heat down to low. Cook gently for 20 minutes until little holes appear all over the surface of the cooked rice and the grains are tender.

4 Fluff up the rice with a fork and transfer it to a warmed serving dish. Sprinkle the chopped almonds and pistachios on top, if using, and serve.

15-MINUTE COUSCOUS

225g (8oz) couscous

75g (3oz) dates, roughly chopped

large pinch of saffron threads

40g (1½oz) butter

25g (1oz) flaked almonds

serves 4

preparation time: 5 minutes

soaking time: 10 minutes

per serving: 350 cals, 12g fat, 55g carbohydrate

All too often when cooking couscous, you end up with a soggy mess. Follow our guide to guarantee perfectly separate grains. _Illustrated._

1 Put the couscous, dates, saffron and 25g (1oz) of the butter in a bowl. Add 300ml (½ pint) boiling water, season and stir to mix everything together. Cover and leave to soak for 10 minutes or until all the water is absorbed and the couscous is soft.

2 Line a 300ml (½ pint) bowl with clingfilm. Spoon in a quarter of the couscous and press down firmly. Invert a dinner plate on to the couscous and turn out, discarding the clingfilm. Repeat three times with the rest of the couscous.

3 Fry the almonds in the remaining butter until golden and scatter over the couscous. Serve.

SWEET POTATO MASH

2 medium potatoes (around 400g/14oz), such as
   King Edward, cut into chunks

900g (2lb) sweet potatoes, cut into chunks

50g (2oz) butter

serves 6

preparation time: 10 minutes

cooking time: 20 minutes

per serving: 240 cals, 7g fat, 42g carbohydrate

The mix of regular and sweet potatoes gives this mash a rounded, earthy taste. It is lovely with lamb chops.

1 Put both types of potato in a large pan of cold, salted water. Cover and bring to the boil, then simmer, half covered, for 15–20 minutes until tender.

2 Drain well, add the butter and season well with salt and freshly ground black pepper. Mash until smooth.

PUDDINGS AND SWEET FIXES

In this chapter you will find a whole variety of puddings and sweet fixes. All can be made in under half an hour. You will see that many are based around fruit, and some are virtually instant. Others are more luxurious and homely, and so are ideal for dinner parties or for when the family is all together.

STICKY MAPLE SYRUP PINEAPPLE

1 large pineapple, peeled and cut
   lengthways into quarters
200ml (7fl oz) maple syrup

serves 4
preparation time: 10 minutes
cooking time: 5 minutes
per serving: 230 cals, nil fat, 57g carbohydrate

Maple syrup makes a brilliant ready-made sauce. Warm it with wedges of pineapple for a sticky pud that tastes wonderful – and it's fat free, too!

1 Cut away the central woody core from each pineapple quarter. Slice each lengthways into four to make 16 wedges.
2 Pour the maple syrup into a large non-stick frying pan and heat for 2 minutes. Add the pineapple and fry for 3 minutes, turning once, until warmed through.
3 Arrange the pineapple on serving plates, drizzle the maple syrup over and around it and serve.

AMARETTI WITH LEMON MASCARPONE

juice of ¼ lemon, plus the rind pared from
   ¼ lemon, white skin removed, and sliced
   finely into long strips
1tbsp golden caster sugar, plus a little extra to sprinkle
50g (2oz) mascarpone
13 single Amaretti biscuits

makes 12
preparation time: 15 minutes
cooking time: 5 minutes
per serving: 20 cals, 1g fat, 2g carbohydrate

Traditional Italian almond biscuits provide the perfect base for a luscious creamy topping. For a pretty finishing touch, decorate the tops with some fine strips of crystallized lemon.

1 Put the lemon juice in a small pan. Add the sugar and dissolve over a low heat. Add the finely sliced lemon rind and cook for 1–2 minutes – it will curl up. Lift out, using a slotted spoon, and put on to a sheet of baking parchment, reserving the syrup. Sprinkle with golden caster sugar to coat.
2 Beat the mascarpone in a bowl to soften, then stir in the sugar syrup.
3 Crush one of the Amaretti biscuits and put to one side, ready to dust.
4 Put a blob of mascarpone on to each remaining Amaretti biscuit, then top with a couple of strips of the crystallized lemon peel. Sprinkle over the crushed Amaretti crumbs.

tip: *If you're short of time, buy a packet of crystallized lemon slices and use these to decorate the Amaretti biscuits. Alternatively, you can simply decorate each biscuit with a little finely grated lemon zest.*

CHOCOLATE CRÊPES WITH A BOOZY SAUCE

100g (3½oz) plain flour, sifted

1 medium egg

300ml (½ pint) milk

sunflower oil for frying

100g (3½oz) unsalted butter

100g (3½oz) light brown muscovado sugar, plus extra
   to sprinkle

4tbsp brandy

50g (2oz) dark chocolate, minimum 70% cocoa solids,
   roughly chopped

serves 4

preparation time: 5 minutes, plus 20 minutes standing

cooking time: 10 minutes

per serving: 550 cals, 32g fat, 52g carbohydrate

Simple and quick sumptuous pancakes to enjoy on Shrove Tuesday or any other day of the year!

1 Put the flour and a pinch of salt in a bowl, make a well in the centre and add the egg. Use a balloon whisk to mix the egg with a little of the flour, then gradually add the milk to make a smooth batter. Cover and leave to stand for about 20 minutes.
2 Pour the batter into a jug. Heat 1tsp oil in a 23cm (9in) pancake pan, then pour 100ml (3½ fl oz) batter into the centre of the pan. Tip the pan around so the mixture coats the base and fry for 1–2 minutes until golden underneath. Use a palette knife to flip over and fry on the other side. Tip on to a plate, cover with a piece of greaseproof paper and repeat with the remaining batter, using more oil as necessary.
3 Put the butter in a frying pan with the sugar and melt over a low heat to mix together. Add the brandy and stir.
4 Divide the chocolate between the crêpes. Fold each in half, then in half again.
5 Slide each pancake into the pan and cook for 3–4 minutes to melt the chocolate, turning halfway through to coat with the sauce. Serve the crêpes drizzled with sauce and sprinkled with extra sugar.

CHOCOLATE RICE KRISPIES

150g (5oz) unsalted butter, plus extra to grease

350g (12oz) milk chocolate, such as Green & Black's,
   broken into pieces

75g (3oz) golden syrup

200g (7oz) Rice Krispies

makes 18

preparation time: 10 minutes

cooking time: 5 minutes

per krispie: 220 cals, 13g fat, 25g carbohydrate

These are incredibly easy to make and so moreish they'll disappear in a flash! The butter, chocolate and golden syrup need to be melted gently over a low heat.

1 Grease a shallow 20.5 × 20.5cm (8 × 8in) tin.
2 Put the butter in a large pan, add the milk chocolate and golden syrup, then melt over a low heat.
3 Add the Rice Krispies and mix together until the cereal is thoroughly coated. Spoon into the tin and push into the corners. Use the back of a wet spatula to level the surface, then leave to cool.
4 Use a palette knife to ease the edges of the cake away from the tin, then invert on to a board. Cut into fingers, wrap in clingfilm and store in the fridge for up to a week, otherwise the cakes will turn soft.

WICKED CHOCOLATE SLICES

225g (8oz) butter
3tbsp golden syrup
50g (2oz) cocoa, sifted
300g packet digestive biscuits, crushed
400g (14oz) dark chocolate, broken into squares

makes 20
preparation time: 10 minutes, plus 30 minutes setting
cooking time: 2 minutes
per serving: 280 cals, 18g fat, 26g carbohydrate

These scrumptious morsels need no cooking and will be gone in no time. *Illustrated.*

1 Put the butter, golden syrup and cocoa in a bowl. Melt in a microwave on High for around 20 seconds or until melted (or melt in a pan on a very low heat). Mix everything together.
2 Remove the mixture from the heat and stir in the crushed biscuits. Mix together well until thoroughly coated in the cocoa mixture, crushing down any large pieces of digestive biscuit as you do so.
3 Spoon the mixture into a greased 25.5 × 16.5cm (10 × 6½in) rectangular tin. Cool, cover and chill for 30 minutes.
4 Put the chocolate in a bowl and melt in a microwave on High for 1 minute 40 seconds or over a pan of simmering water. Stir once, pour the chocolate over the biscuit base, then put the tin in the fridge for 30 minutes or until the topping has set. Cut in half lengthways, then cut each section into 10 slices.

MARINATED STRAWBERRIES

350g (12oz) strawberries
Juice of ½ lemon
2tbsp golden caster sugar

serves 4
preparation time: 5 minutes
per serving; 100cals, 0g fat; 26g carbohydrates
  (without ice cream)

A delicious and easy summer dish for when strawberries and abundant and in season.

1 Hull the strawberries and cut in half, if large. Put in a bowl with the lemon juice and caster sugar. Stir to mix, then set aside for 30 minutes. Serve with vanilla ice cream.

TROPICAL FRUIT SALAD

4 passion fruit

100g (3½oz) golden caster sugar

50ml (2fl oz) white rum or Malibu

zest and juice of 1 lime

125g (4oz) punnet of cranberries

1 pineapple, peeled, cored and sliced lengthways

1 papaya, peeled, halved, deseeded and sliced
   lengthways

1 large ripe mango, peeled, halved and cut into slices

1 large banana, sliced on the diagonal

serves 8

preparation time: 20 minutes, plus 30
   minutes marinating

cooking time: 7 minutes

per serving: 120 cals, trace of fat, 28g carbohydrate

There's nothing quite as refreshing as a fruit salad. Here we combine tropical fruits and cranberries with a rum and lime syrup for added zing.

1 Rest a sieve on a small pan, halve the passion fruit and scrape the seeds into the sieve. Stir with a wooden spoon to extract the juice. Discard the seeds.

2 Put the sugar, rum, lime zest and juice in the pan and heat gently to make a syrup. Add the cranberries and cook on a medium heat for 5 minutes. Allow to cool.

3 Put the pineapple, papaya, mango and banana in a large bowl. Pour the cranberries and syrup over the fruit. Leave to marinate at room temperature for at least 30 minutes to let the flavours develop before serving.

FRUIT SALAD

2 peaches

1 ripe mango

4 passion fruits

serves 4

preparation time: 10 minutes

per serving; 60cals, 0g fat; 14g carbohydrates

A simple fruit salad for when summer fruits are available and in season.

1 Halve and stone the peaches and finely slice. Put in a bowl. Peel the mango, then cut off the flesh from either side of the stone. Discard the stone and finely slice the fruit. Add to the bowl with the passion fruit seeds and juice. Gently mix everything together and serve.

CHERRY YOGURT CRUSH

400g can stoned cherries, drained,
  or 450g fresh cherries, stoned
500g Greek yogurt
150g pack ratafia biscuits
4tbsp cherry brandy

serves 4
preparation time: 10 minutes, plus 15 minutes chilling
per serving: 390 cals, 14g fat, 51g carbohydrate

Layer oh-so-creamy Greek yogurt with ripe juicy cherries, a splash of cherry brandy and crunchy almond-infused ratafia biscuits for a very special dessert. For a healthy version, make with low-fat Greek yogurt instead of the full-fat version.

1 Take four glass pots or elegant glasses – each should hold around 400ml (14fl oz). Spoon some cherries into the base of each. Top with a dollop of yogurt, some ratafia biscuits and a drizzle of cherry brandy.
2 Continue layering up each glass until all the ingredients are used up. Chill for 15 minutes – 2 hours before serving.

CHOCOLATE POTS

200g bar plain chocolate (70% cocoa)
zest of 1 orange
284ml carton double cream
150g (5oz) caster sugar
50ml (2fl oz) orange liqueur
3 large egg whites
1 large orange, cut into 10 wedges

serves 10
preparation time: 15 minutes, plus chilling
cooking time: 5 minutes
per serving: 310 cals, 21g fat, 24g carbohydrate

Seriously rich, with a touch of tangy citrus, this is the perfect dessert for confirmed chocoholics. They're best eaten within a couple of hours of making, before the chocolate becomes too firmly set and cloying, but there should be no lack of takers!

1 Melt the chocolate in a heatproof bowl over simmering water, then remove and stir in the zest. Whip the cream with 100g (3½oz) sugar and the liqueur until thick. Whisk the egg whites in a clean bowl until soft peaks form, then gradually whisk in the remaining sugar until stiff.
2 Fold the chocolate into the cream – the mixture will thicken – and continue until well mixed. Beat a spoonful of the egg whites into the mixture to loosen it, then add the remaining whites and fold them in thoroughly.
3 Spoon the chocolate mousse into 10 small ramekin dishes or coffee cups.
4 Chill the pots for 1 hour, then serve each one with a wedge of fresh orange.

VANILLA TIRAMISU

200g tub mascarpone

1 vanilla pod

450ml (¾ pint) warm, strong black coffee

4 medium egg yolks

75g (3oz) caster sugar

284ml carton double cream, whipped into soft peaks

100ml (4fl oz) grappa

200g packet sponge fingers or savoiardi biscuits

1 level tbsp cocoa powder to dust

serves 10

preparation time: 20 minutes, plus chilling

per serving: 380 cals, 27g fat, 27g carbohydrate

We guarantee you'll think this is the most gorgeous version you've ever tasted, and it's deceptively easy. It also improves in flavour if you make it a day in advance. *Illustrated.*

1 Put the mascarpone in a bowl.

2 Cut the vanilla pod in half lengthways, scrape out the seeds and add them to the mascarpone.

3 Add the vanilla pod to the coffee and pour the liquid into a shallow dish to allow the flavours to mingle.

4 In a large bowl, whisk the yolks and sugar until pale and thick, then whisk in the mascarpone until smooth.

5 Fold the cream and grappa into the mascarpone mixture.

6 Take half of the sponge fingers and dip each in turn into the coffee mixture, then arrange in the base of a 2.4 litre (4½ pint) shallow dish. Spread a layer of mascarpone mixture over, then dip the remaining sponge fingers in the coffee and arrange on top. Finish with a final layer of mascarpone mixture.

7 Cover and chill before serving. Dust with the cocoa and use a spatula to serve on individual plates.

NECTARINES AND APRICOTS WITH PISTACHIOS

6 apricots, halved, stoned and sliced

2 nectarines, halved, stoned and sliced

2tbsp runny honey

50g (2oz) shelled pistachio nuts, chopped

serves 4

preparation time: 5 minutes

per serving; 160cals, 7g fat; 22g carbohydrates

This combination of fruit, honey and yogurt is ideal for dessert of for breakfast.

1 Arrange the apricots and nectarines on a plate and drizzle over the honey. Scatter over the pistachio nuts and serve with Greek yogurt.

INDEX